Moving with Change

Rowena Pattee was a close student of Shunryu Suzuki Roshi, Zen Master of Tassajara Monastery, California, from 1963 until his death in 1971. Her studies of the *I Ching* pre-date her Zen practice. She is currently on the faculty of the California Institute of Integral Studies in San Francisco and is the founder of the Creative Harmonics Institute in Mount Shasta, California. She promotes conferences on culture-making, shamanism, creativity, sacred sites and interdisciplinary methods. She is an artist, film-maker, architectural designer and teacher. She has a M.F.A. in art and film-making and a Ph.D. in Religious Studies with emphasis on cross-cultural mythology. Rowena Pattee has written several other books, including *Song to Thee: Divine Androgyne* (1973), and numerous articles, including 'Shaman's Path' (1988). Rowena Pattee is featured in *Shape Shifters: Shaman Women in Contemporary Society* (Arkana, 1987).

ROWENA PATTEE

MOVING WITH CHANGE

A Women's Reintegration of the I Ching
Foreword by José Argüelles

ARKANA

ARKANA

Published by the Penguin Group
27 Wrights Lane, London W8 5TZ, England
Viking Penguin Inc., 40 West 23rd Street, New York, New York 10010, USA
Penguin Books Australia Ltd, Ringwood, Victoria, Australia
Penguin Books Canada Ltd, 2801 John Street, Markham, Ontario, Canada L3R 1B4
Penguin Books (NZ) Ltd, 182–190 Wairau Road, Auckland 10, New Zealand

Penguin Books Ltd, Registered Offices: Harmondsworth, Middlesex, England

First published by Arkana 1986
3 5 7 9 10 8 6 4 2

Filmset in 11 on 13pt Sabon
Printed and bound in Great Britain by
Cox & Wyman Ltd, Reading

This book is dedicated to my mother

Eleanor Kryder

who has always been a great support
and continues to be by finding her true
way of life and whose spirit shines
brightly in the limitless

Contents

PART III
Commentaries on *I Ching* and the Golden Hexagrams

Appendices

Foreword

The pristine binary language of *I Ching*, whose sixty-four key words or hexagrams correspond precisely to the sixty-four codons of DNA, is essentially the language of the future.

But the future is nothing distant. Just as the DNA codons comprising the language of universal life are embedded in all living forms, so the binary constellations of *I Ching* represent a future present tense the vocabulary of which has already constructed the forms of nature and culture that constitute the past. Because there is a dire contemporary need to recollect this perennial truth in its most essential structural form, *I Ching* continues to assert itself into the present moment.

The question arises when confronted with *I Ching*: how to derive the best use of it? Once we clear away the fact that *I Ching* is not intrinsically Chinese, but, like silicon chips, universal in form and application, then an approach may be made that renders it useful. For most people, however, who consult *I Ching* by a throw of the coins, the use is highly limited by a reliance on the verbal constructs of the interpreters, as often as not Richard Wilhelm and Cary Baynes. As insightful as the interpretations of these two men might be, to rely on their words alone is rather to miss the point. *I Ching is a multi-dimensional language that functions as a result of an intuitive apprehension of the binary structures constituting its vocabulary.*

It is for this reason that one of the traditional commentaries of *I Ching* describes it thus:

> In it are included the forms and the scope of everything in the heavens and on earth, so that nothing escapes it. In it all things everywhere are completed, so that none is missing. Therefore, by means of it we can penetrate the tao of day and night, and so understand it. Therefore the spirit is bound to no one place, nor the Book of Changes to any one form.

Understanding *I Ching* in this light, one can warmly and with open, inquisitive heart and mind welcome the appearance of Rowena Pattee's astonishingly creative *Moving with Change: A Woman's Reintegration of the I Ching*. Beginning with her presentation of the Golden Hexagrams and their derivations, Rowena Pattee weaves and amplifies upon a tapestry so rich in information and so penetrating in its application, that one can only come away from it realizing that here, indeed, is a distillation of the most genuine contemplative life experience.

As coherently scientific as it is originally artistic, for the thoughtful student of *I Ching* Rowena Pattee's presentation will undoubtedly become a well-worn reference. Beyond that, even for the more casual student, this volume should become a precise tool unlocking innumerable pathways of intuitive learning.

In fact, as much as it is a manifestation of intuitive learning, *Moving with Change* is equally a manual on how to become more intuitively resonant, and as a consequence, more aware, present, and universally compassionate. In other words, *Moving with Change* is nothing less than a valuable guidebook for becoming the kind of complete person this planet requires in order to attain its fullness in the Golden Light of a present that has always been.

José Argüelles, Ph.D.
Boulder

Introduction

Moving with Change is an outgrowth of the ageless wisdom of the *I Ching* (Chinese 'Book of Changes'), distilled and adapted for our own times in twenty-two years of intense life and careful reflection. It is easy to use and the reader can receive much benefit through trials and choice-points of life if an honest friend is wanted. This book can be that friend and will stand by you in utmost constancy through change. Such constancy is a living truth which is easy unless one resists it.

The truth of constancy in change comes down the ages and yet is always eternal. This book reveals methods to *Move with Change*. In using this book, the reader may discover a new attitude toward change itself. When one fully understands that change is the only constant in life, we can see that this book is a mirror which reflects the pattern and rhythm of transformations we all move through. That we live in critical times of personal, national and global change makes it all the more imperative to learn how to *Move with Change*. Once one sees change as inevitable and steady, then we may loosen our hold and attachment to preconceived attitudes, forms, and codes of being. We may then be immediately and spontaneously liberated from the suffering that comes from clinging to *anything* too solidly.

This liberation enables our intuition to develop. Intuition has the same properties as seeds. When planted in fertile ground, the seeds will grow. The fertile ground of one's being is a living state in which the seeds of truth can grow naturally. By using this book the reader's intuition about his/her own life can unfold like a flower.

The fruits of one's life naturally grow when the 'Humble Vigilance' and 'Inner Truth' (the essential meaning of 'Dragon and Tiger' symbols used in this book) are applied to daily life. Whether the fruits are bitter or sweet depends on the nourishment they have received. The 'images', 'judgments' and 'lines' presented in this book are a kind of nourishment and if

1

one can accept and digest what life brings and use this book as a mirror, one's heart and mind can then shine and radiate nourishment to others . . . like golden apples.

The most practical way of using this book is to go directly to the methods in Part I, cast an oracle by any method you choose, then refer to one or more of the sixty-four 'hexagrams' relevant in Part II. The 'hexagrams' are a name used for the six-line configurations and their associated meanings. Reflect on the images and the meaning of the words to witness clearly what you are experiencing. For example, if you really want to know whether to apply for such and such a job, to change your attitude about a person who annoys you, or even whether to repair the roof now or later, the Tiger and Dragon oracle will make a clear, specific suggestion for you. Whether you accept it or not is entirely up to you.

Gradually, as you use the book, you will get to know the oracle like an old wise friend with a sense of humour, but an old friend who is unmercifully honest with you, though strictly confidential. If you can trust this old friend, a pathway opens which can give more and more clarity and consequently happiness and humor at the dilemmas and difficulties and confusions of being human and living between what the Chinese call 'Heaven and Earth.'

Having been a conscious agent for the *I Ching* for twenty-two years in this life, I have become very well acquainted with the oracle and 'it' has given me permission, even a mandate, to present it with 'Tiger and Dragon' images to help contemporary men and women to reconcile their differences and gain insight into the 'yin' and 'yang' or feminine and masculine qualities in each person.

Every person, according to this oracle, whether female or male, is androgynous in various inner ways and tendencies. Consequently, there is a slightly different emphasis in each 'hexagram' for men and for women. This difference is based on the subtle energy current the Taoists call *Ch'i*, the Hindus call *Prana* and the Sufis call *Baraka*. It doesn't matter what you call it. The point is that this energy current is the source of our vital life. It is subtle nourishment. It is so subtle we don't even notice it and yet if it were taken away we would be dead!

Harmony in this life consists in knowing how to move with this current, when to be still and when to be active, when to pivot and when to leap, when to sit and when to dance. In practical life this means whether to call so and so and attempt to reconcile, or whether to hold one's point until it is heard; whether to let your property go or whether to fight; whether to remain inward or express oneself outwardly. Listening to the oracle is not fooling ourselves. It requires complete honesty and active response to the mirror of truth *Moving with Change* offers. It is knowing when to ask a question and when to act on the answer. It is knowing when to retreat and when to follow, when to work on something that has been spoiled and when to leave it alone. It is learning when to change our 'normal' habitual patterns of thinking, feeling and acting.

Moving with Change is not a fortune-telling device, but rather a path to heightened clarity and the ability to transform into our true, deep spontaneous Self. When one truly lives in the presence of the present, the full potentiality of the past and future are present too! The intention here is not only to grasp an answer, but to become open to our own most basic questions. Some basic questions might be decisions concerning the direction of one's career, how to become more flexible or firm in one's marriage, and how to accept criticism from others. There is no limit to questions, but the only way the oracle can provide a true mirror of one's life is if questions come from the core of our being and from the utmost honesty and willingness to learn and change.

Transition and change are based on imbalance and such imbalances can be dynamic, in which case they will again come into equilibrium, or they can be static, in which case there is danger of a chronic imbalance. When we lose our balance there is naturally a kind of death. Following death is a rebirth and growth. How to move through change is dying to be reborn through an increasing awareness of what I call the 'Silver River of Tao'.

This Silver River of Tao can be illustrated by a story told by Chuang-tzu (Chuang-tzu 19, tr. H.A. Giles (1) pp. 233–4):

Yen Yuan said to Confucius, 'When I crossed over the Shang-shen rapid, the boatman managed his craft with marvelous skill. I asked him if handling a boat could be learnt. "It can", replied he. "The way of those who know how to keep you afloat is more like sinking you. They row as if the boat wasn't there." I enquired what this meant, but he would not tell me. May I ask its signification?'

'It means,' answered Confucius, 'that such a man is oblivious of the water around him. He regards the rapid as though dry land. He looks upon an upset as an ordinary cart accident. And if a man can but be impervious to capsizings and accidents in general, whither should he not be able comfortably to go?'

Using *Moving with Change* is easy with such an attitude. The Silver River of Tao is the effortless effort of learning about the interpenetration of visible and invisible realms, of change and constancy. It teaches one to be a gentle and accepting warrior, a warrior without a mask, rigid weapons or aggressive way. Such fearlessness becomes possible because the Silver River of Tao is actually a perfect harmony which is in the background of our daily deaths and rebirths ceaselessly changing. Using *Moving with Change* is having confidence in a basic harmony of the Silver River of Tao while daily being confronted with the vicissitudes of life.

The images, judgments and lines in this book are like specific eddies or rivulets, giving insight which enables us to go through whatever is needed with acceptance, embracing life whole-heartedly. Thereby the condition changes. If we resist, both the condition and suffering continue. This is ignorance that can be swept aside by our own insights through using *Moving with Change*. Even though all individual beings are under the influence of the subtle etheric network of the Silver River of Tao, if we do not realize it, we can obscure our aware connection with the cosmic administrative system. Without this awareness, we are controlled and tossed in the waves of life.

The order of the universe does not tolerate heaped up debts and malevolence, either to nature or to human beings, without severe penalties. As a world we are beginning to feel some penalties as well as rewards of past thoughts and actions and can be grateful for it. To understand the flow of the Silver River of Tao through *Moving with Change* is to learn to move with equanimity (non-reaction) on the white waters of trans-formation. *Moving with Change* is a key to the critical transition we are experiencing in these latter days of the twentieth century. *Moving with Change* is a timely book to help us 'flow with it' and realize both our individuality and our oneness. I am grateful for being an agent for my wise old humorous friend, the 'Tiger and Dragon' oracle, to speak through.

One might well ask, how is it possible for there to be a 'new' *I Ching* or something called a Tiger-Dragon oracle based on the traditional *I Ching*?

I can only humbly say that I have been absorbed gently and yet powerfully by the wisdom of the *I Ching*, to the way of change, and consequently am so changed that the constancies through change speak through this 'Tiger and Dragon' oracle.

There is no attempt here to replace the standard *I Ching* in its numerous translations. It is, rather, an outgrowth of it, just as various commentaries have been added throughout the thousands of years the *I Ching* has been used.

If the reader develops an interest on how this oracle is an extension for modern times of the ancient *I Ching*, then go to Part III of this book and read the Commentaries and Appendices. If you are already an *I Ching* scholar or student, then the Commentaries might interest you in showing how the hexagrams in *Moving with Change* are linked with Taoist Yoga and the Silver River of Tao I have mentioned.

PART I

Methods of the Oracle

— 1 —
Ways of casting the oracle

THE QUESTION

Allowing the present situation to be formulated is a method of bringing the unconscious mind into consciousness. The oracle answers the real question of the questioner's being, not surface thoughts and curiosities. It is important to get to the root of your deepest desires and fears to find the source of your question and then formulate it.

Questions may be personal, global, practical, spiritual, psychological, etc. Write down your questions as they come to you and then review them, penetrating to their common root. Then rephrase the question including specific people, situations, timing, etc., and inquire about the attitude to take. You can't expect yes or no answers. Therefore don't ask yes or no questions. You can ask about the direction of your present situation, its effect on others, whether to go ahead or pause, whether to include others or remain alone, etc.

The oracle will give a response to the vibrational reality of your present question as it represents your present state and your tendencies towards the future. It is helpful to write down the question, date it and include the oracle cast in your diary.

CHANCE AND INTERFERENCE PATTERNS

It may seem ridiculous to the rational mind that a chance throw of coins or sticks or cards can bear any apparent accurate relevance to one's life situation. It might, however, be compared to the creation of a hologram where neither the original object nor holographic image bear any resemblance to the interference pattern which stores the vibratory information to make possible the reconstruction of the image. The 'chance' throwing of coins, sticks or cards is analogous to the interference pattern from which the hexagram can be constructed and interpreted.

The archetypal patterns permeate what we call a Global Psi Field and are analogous to the original object of a hologram. The image and qualities of the hexagrams are analogous to the holographic image to be interpreted according to one's level of knowledge, insight and intuition. Flow with it. What is often called 'chance' is simply an incomprehensible law. Is anything by chance?

THE COIN METHOD

Whether you use three old Chinese bronze coins or three pennies or any other currencies does not matter as long as you reserve them for consulting the oracle.

First determine whether 'heads' or 'tails' is a 3 or a 2 (the oracle needs to know this!). If heads is a 2 and tails a 3, then:

$$
\begin{array}{lll}
H & H & T = 7 = \text{---} \\
2 + 2 + 3
\end{array}
$$

$$
\begin{array}{lll}
T & T & H = 8 = \text{-- --} \\
3 + 3 + 2
\end{array}
$$

$$
\begin{array}{lll}
H & H & H = 6 = \text{--×--} \\
2 + 2 + 2
\end{array}
$$

$$
\begin{array}{lll}
T & T & T = 9 = \text{--○--} \\
3 + 3 + 3
\end{array}
$$

Shake the three coins in your hands until you feel it is time to 'throw' them. Let them fall to the floor (or table, mountain-top, phone-booth, etc.) and read the first throw as the first (bottom) line of the hexagram. Six such 'throws' will yield the hexagram reading from the bottom upward.

THE STALK METHOD

The Chinese used yarrow stalks, but any wooden sticks will do as long as they are reserved only for consulting the oracle. The stick method is likely to be more accurate than the coin method, based on the amount of vibratory interaction in creating the interference pattern. You will need 50 (perfect number in Chinese numerology) sticks.

First you put one of the sticks aside, using 49 (7 × 7 = yang).

Divide the 49 sticks into two piles. Take one stick from the right-hand pile and place it between the little finger and ring finger of the left hand. Then take the left-hand pile and count off the sticks by fours until there are four or fewer sticks left. Place these sticks between the ring finger and middle finger and proceed to count off the sticks of the right-hand pile by fours.

The remainder will either be 5 or 9. Leave these 5 or 9 sticks aside and repeat the procedure with the remaining sticks two more times. The next two countings will yield either 4 or 8 remaining sticks.

Write down the number as you proceed, assigning the values as follows:

5 = 3   9 = 2
4 = 3   8 = 2

Thus you may have any one of the following combinations:

5 + 4 + 4 = 9 = —o—
(3)   (3)   (3)

9 + 8 + 8 = 6 = —×—
(2)   (2)   (2)

$\left.\begin{array}{l} 9 + 8 + 4 \\ (2)\ (2)\ (3) \\ \\ 5 + 8 + 4 \\ (3)\ (2)\ (3) \\ \\ 9 + 4 + 8 \\ (2)\ (3)\ (2) \end{array}\right\}$ = 7 = ———

$\left.\begin{array}{l} 9 + 4 + 4 \\ (2)\ (3)\ (3) \\ \\ 5 + 4 + 8 \\ (3)\ (3)\ (2) \\ \\ 5 + 8 + 4 \\ (3)\ (2)\ (3) \end{array}\right\}$ = 8 = — —

Proceed in the same manner with all six lines starting always with the bottom line. This will take eighteen divisions of the sticks (three for each line times six for each hexagram equals eighteen).

SEED OR PEBBLE METHOD

Another method of obtaining a hexagram is to use tiny pebbles or seeds. The Chinese advise using the seeds of Cassia tora, which are called 'wise decision' seeds. But rice, wheat or any other seeds or tiny stones will do.

Pick up a few seeds or pebbles between your middle finger and thumb, and place them on a clean sheet of white paper or light cloth. Do this six times in succession, starting from the bottom and working upward, leaving six little piles.

Now count the number of seeds in each cluster. If there is an even number of seeds (2, 4, 6, 8, etc.) then the line is yin. If there is an odd number of seeds (1, 3, 5, 7, etc.) the line is yang. To find the changing line in this method, pick up a pile of seeds or pebbles and count the number in the pile. If it is 6 or less, use that number as the number of the changing line. If you have more than 6 in your pile, subtract by 6s to find the number remaining. If you have 11 seeds, then $11 - 6 = 5$. Then read the fifth line as specific to your situation.

A similar method is to make marks, dots or holes on paper, sand, etc., in six rows and counting the odd and even numbers.

FINDING THE HEXAGRAM

In the traditional method, hexagrams are made of two trigrams. Look up the lower trigram (the first three lines from the bottom) and upper trigram (lines four, five and six) in the chart in Appendix 3 and look where the rows and columns join to find the correct hexagram. Reflect on the image, the Tiger and Dragon oracle judgment and allow your intuition to surface like a dream. This can give you further insights into your situation.

INTUITIVE METHODS

As long as the intention and intuition of the questioner is clear, various methods of using the oracle can be used effectively. Even recognition of hexagrams in the landscape, marks on trees, patterns of cars on the street, or expressions on faces are valid. It depends on the knowledge and wisdom of the questioner. If something reminds you of a hexagram, look at the image and read the judgment to receive insights on your question.

CARD METHODS

One of the simplest methods of using the Tiger and Dragon oracle cards is to shuffle them and cut into three piles face down, reassemble into one pile and draw three cards off the top. Read the first card as the present, the second card as the past and the third card as the future:

```
┌─────────┐   ┌─────────┐   ┌─────────┐
│         │   │         │   │         │
│ present │   │  past   │   │ future  │
│         │   │         │   │         │
│         │   │         │   │         │
│    1    │   │    2    │   │    3    │
└─────────┘   └─────────┘   └─────────┘
```

A trend of destiny can be seen by this method which can be helpful in directives.

'Tiger and Dragon I Ching Cards' are available; see p. 297 for suppliers.

TEN CARDS

Another card method is that used in the Tarot. After shuffling and cutting into three piles, put the cards together face down and proceed to take ten cards and interpret as follows:

Card 1   *Present*. The questioner and present atmosphere.
Card 2   *Immediate influence*. That which is just coming into the situation.
Card 3   *Destiny*. The goal based on the present situation.
Card 4   *Distant past influence*. Karmic foundation embodied in the questioner.
Card 5   *Recent past influence*. Conditions passing out of the situation.
Card 6   *Future influence*. Tendency of unfoldment.
Card 7   *Questioner*. Your present state and circumstances. This card has more perspective than card 1.
Card 8   *Environment*. Your influence on other people and circumstances and how this in turn affects you.
Card 9   *Deep inner feelings*. Motives that may be unconscious to you.
Card 10 *Outcome*. The culmination from all previous tendencies.

YIN AND YANG EIGHT-CARD METHOD*

In this method, the questioner can learn about the active (creative) and passive (receptive) aspects with respect to the question. This includes a differentiation of the weaknesses and strengths of the questioner's physical, psychological and spiritual life.

First shuffle the cards well with the question or state of your integral life in mind. Then divide all the cards into three piles, moving the piles of cards towards you. The first pile (furthest away from you) represents your spiritual life, the second pile represents your psychological (emotional-psychic-mental) life and the pile nearest you represents your physical life.

Now shuffle the first pile, being aware of your spiritual aims and questions and then divide it into two piles. The pile you place on the right represents the yang (active, creative) aspect of your spiritual life, while the pile on the left represents the yin (passive, receptive) aspect of your spiritual life.

Now shuffle the right pile (yang) and draw one card off the top and place it on the upper right while you place the remainder of the pile aside.

Now shuffle the left pile (yin) and draw one card off the bottom and place it on the upper left while you place the remainder of the pile aside with the first remainder.

Do not yet look at the face of the cards. The next step is to shuffle the middle pile concentrating on your psychic, mental and emotional life. Divide this pile into right and left and follow the same instructions as given for the first pile, but place the right and left cards in the middle. The remainder are to be put aside with the remainders of the first pile.

Now shuffle the pile nearest you concentrating on your physical life, your health, environment, financial resources, etc. Following the same instructions as given for the first and second piles, placing the right and left cards on the lower right and left.

You should now have a right (yang) and left (yin) single card for your spirit, psyche and body. Now take the pile of cards which remain and shuffle them thinking of your main question or aim. Spread these fifty-eight cards out before you and select one which resonates most strongly or seems to 'speak' to you. Place this card above your right and left spirit cards. This card is the 'source-effect' or overall ruling pattern of this reading. It tells you both what your aims are and possible consequences.

Now select another card from the remaining fifty-seven cards and place it below the right and left body cards, thinking of the methods you might take to fulfill your destiny or purpose. This is the 'agent-process' card which indicates the means you might use to accomplish what is indicated in the 'source-effect' card.

The arrangement of your cards should look like this:

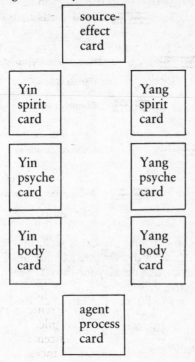

Now turn over the cards and interpret according to the positions given above. The active (yang) side can be interpreted to mean what you might actively initiate with respect to the given aspect. The passive (yin) side can be interpreted to mean what will happen to you or what you will receive or perhaps what will be unconscious to you.

*This arrangement is based on the 'androgynous Tarot spread' of Angeles Arrien.

SEVENTEEN-CARD HOLISTIC ALIGNMENT METHOD

With this method you will find how your energy centers (chakras) are aligned with respect to the triple functions of 1 active, 2 neutral and 3 passive. This is based on the five elements of the Chinese Fu Hsi order (see Commentary 1) and is the pristine harmonious order of the chakras:

Metal			Mind, discrimination (head center)	ultra-violet
Fire			Perception, formation (throat center)	blue
Wood			Psyche, intuition (heart center)	green
Water			Feelings, emotions (navel center)	red-orange
Earth			Body, primary vitality (root center)	infra-red (heat)

In this method, after shuffling the cards well, divide them into five piles, placing the most distant pile as your head center, the next pile moving towards you as your throat, heart, navel and root centers, respectively.

There are two ways to lay out the fifteen cards depending on whether you presently need purification (moving from matter to spirit) or whether you need grounding and the power to manifest (spirit to matter).

Purification direction

For purification the layout of the fifteen cards moves from the root center up to the head center and begins from left to right.

Shuffle the pile nearest you 'tuning in' to your energy and vitality, your body, resources, environment and material patterns as the ground of your being. Spread out this pile into three, beginning with the left as follows:

(left)	(middle)	(right)
Reflective	Essential	Projective
(passive)	(neutral)	(active)

The subtle energy of ch'i comes in at the left and moves right through the neutral column in the root center; but in the navel center the current moves from right to left and so on as follows:

5th	Head center	left to right	Metal
4th	Throat center	right to left	Fire
3rd	Heart center	left to right	Wood
2nd	Navel center	right to left	Water
1st	Root center	left to right	Earth

$\rightarrow$

Grounding direction

To diagnose the alignment of your centers for grounding and manifestation of an inspiration or vision, the cards should be spread in the reverse order.

$\rightarrow$

1st	Head center	right to left	Metal
2nd	Throat center	left to right	Fire
3rd	Heart center	right to left	Wood
4th	Navel center	left to right	Water
5th	Root center	right to left	Earth

Whichever direction you use, you should tune in to the pile of cards relevant to the meaning of each center whether 'active', 'neutral' or 'passive'.

When you are laying out the 'active' or 'projective' side remain receptive to all that is *actively radiating* the qualities of your mind, your perceptions, your intuitions, your emotions and your physical life.

When you are laying out the 'neutral' or 'essential' central column, remain receptive to all that is at the real core or center of equilibrium within each of the five centers.

When you are laying out the 'passive' or 'reflective' side, remain receptive to all that is coming into your life, all that is happening to you without your willing it, all that you allow, within each of the five centers.

	Reflective (passive)	Essential (neutral)	Projective (active)
Destiny card			
Head			
Throat			
Heart			
Navel			
Base			
Means of accomplishment			

After you have laid out the fifteen piles, take the top card from each pile and place it face down in the same place while placing all the remaining cards in one great pile. Now take the one great pile and shuffle, tuning in to the whole aim and purpose of your life. Select one card from the whole remaining pile and place it at the top, above the head center. This card is your destiny card and rules the alignment given below it.

Now shuffle the whole remaining pile of cards, tuning in to the means by which you will accomplish your destiny. Select one card from the whole pile and place it below the root center of the whole alignment. This card tells you what process you might take or the *means* of accomplishing your destiny.

Interpret these seventeen cards to find how your various centers are aligned to accomplish your destiny.

ENERGY-CURRENT METHODS

Once one is familiar with patterns, the hexagrams can be seen as energy-currents, beginning with the bottom line and working upwards. Consequently, they can be recognized in sequences of events, the landscape and wave patterns, weaving, etc. Even types of leaves and trees, of species and thought-forms are applicable. But this requires developed intuition and clarity as well as knowledge of the sixty-four hexagrams.

For example, if you are with a friend up on Mt Vision where I live, and see the sun setting over the sea, this is fire over the water or 64 BEFORE COMPLETION. If there are clouds or a fog bank under the sun, it is fire over Heaven, 14 POSSESSION IN GREAT MEASURE.

If you are in a cave and the sea is washing up into it, this is earth over water, 7 THE ARMY; whereas waters rushing down over the earth is 8 UNITY. A mountain above a lake is 41 DECREASE; whereas a mountain reflected in a lake is 31 INFLUENCE. This gives you some idea of landscape interpretation. Other things like a bright bird flying over the earth suggests 35 PROGRESS; whereas a thunderstorm on a hot day suggests 55 ABUNDANCE.

In events, wave patterns or cycles, one can use the qualities of the trigrams given in Commentary 4, suggesting the inception, build-up, ruling over, breaking, dispersing, sinking, flowing back and return of a wave. Series of events often follow this same pattern. To know where you are in a wave or event pattern, is helpful in knowing whether to expect a gathering together or dispersing of energy in the future.

— 2 —
Ways of interpretation

MEANINGS OF STATEMENTS AND IMAGES

After finding the hexagram in the Key (Appendix 3), look up the hexagram in Part II of this book and allow the image to have a direct influence on your subconscious mind. Free associate with the image and write down how it relates to you and your life as you would a dream.

In the beginning, allow your intuition free play and don't doubt. Intuition is spontaneous. Anything that arises bound by rules only is likely to be dead. Intuition brings forth life. It goes wherever its inner awareness takes it, wherever truth or life takes it.

Any suggestions for interpretation given here according to rules are only guide-lines for fresh views. Breaking the *I Ching* into patterns is not analysis, but like the break-up of water thrown into the air by a fountain, it returns to itself refreshed. It is an aerating experience and thereby the water is lightened, ionized and expanded. In essence, nothing is changed and changes are nothing!

When you look up the hexagram you will see a statement below the picture. This is based on relations between elements as sources, agents, processes and effects. Allow the images and the poetic statements below them to act on your imagination. Don't try too hard to figure them out, but just become open and receptive. They have the power to evoke subliminal and subtle aspects in your life which are sources of creativity.

Creativity is the natural flow of life. We need only allow what obstructs it to dissolve away. Creativity flows from effortless energy-currents. Rules and methods are useless in opening intuition, but they may clarify the context. Creative reading means allowing the words to be starting points of an intuitive process.

The first statement below the image is based on the qualities of the eight trigrams and parts of the body in relation to the

Tiger and Dragon (see Commentary 4). An alternation of conscious study of material found in the commentaries and free open intuition will give you the best and most balanced results.

Then read the Judgment and the statement for a man or a woman. This is based on the meanings of the hexagrams attributed to the twelve subtle centers along the central meridian and in the thrusting meridian inside the body (see Commentary 7).

ATTITUDES

The attitude of utmost honesty is necessary to enable the clear harmony of awareness which makes possible accurate interpretation. Then the ego lets go of the projections of the mind and the attachments and habits of the body, if ever so slowly. The shells that the ego built up to protect itself begin to crack and dissolve. Only in this way can the invulnerability of your true Self realize itself.

The universe, life itself, is the teacher. The oracle brings the changes of life into focus, but unless the heart wants the truth, the body and mind cannot accept it and awareness will not shine in consciousness. The true Inner Self is always watching but if we cannot dissolve the barriers the ego has created, there is no awareness of it.

If you have a reaction to the hexagram you have drawn, which is extremely positive or negative, part of your instruction is to observe your own reaction. Likes and dislikes are as irrelevant here as in life. They make no difference except in creating bondages and blockages to full acceptance of the situation and the wisdom of directives given in the oracle.

If you have a tendency to throw the oracle again and again until you get what you want, or a tendency to reject it with a label of nonsense or the like, it indicates a strong reaction. The state of being to realize wholeness from the oracle is a calm, accepting attitude of the utmost sincerity.

It is consciousness which needs to become subtle and clear so that the true Self can reflect in it. The very substance of the body then changes accordingly. The body then becomes present, open, resonating with the entire universe. There are no boundaries. Expansion ¯of consciousness is simultaneously enabling the body to become so subtle that it permeates everything. The body realizes its vibratory resonance with the qualities of the universe. Then one is aware of the universe within oneself. All the changes of body and mind are opportunities to open up this changeless awareness.

The clash between fear and desire, past and future is the root of all suffering. Pain can turn to bliss when accepted. Yin in extremity appears as the cross of weakness and pain, but when accepted, becomes pure open empty feminine compassionate acceptance of the whole universe. Yang in extremity appears as the aura of pleasure and strength which may become over-bearing and grasping, but when accepted, becomes joyous masculine giving and joins with yin in serenity. Serene awareness of both extremes opens deep wells of bliss.

INTERPRETATION BY QUALITIES OF YIN AND YANG

Interpretation of yin and yang lines depends on your know-ledge of the qualities of yin and yang, and of the trigrams (Commentaries 1–4). If you combine this knowledge with honest intention and integral intuition, the immutable quality of your true Self will begin to shine.

Yang has a tendency to move upward (towards Heaven); whereas yin tends to move downward (towards Earth). Consequently with ▬ ▬ there is a tendency to hold together; whereas with ▬▬▬ there is a tendency to move apart. This is particularly true when these relations are between the third and fourth lines attributed to 'Man'. We use this term as inclusive of all persons, men or women.

In 11 PEACE ☷☰ Earth is above Heaven which creates a unity.

In 12 STANDSTILL ☰☷ Heaven is above Earth which creates a separation.

As Richard Wilhelm says (p. 27, *Lectures on the I Ching*): A hexagram may be understood as consisting of two each of the eight basic trigrams. But once ordered, they may also divide as follows:

▬▬▬ 1 Heaven

▬▬ ▬ 2 Man

▬ ▬ 3 Earth

Here the two lower lines are terrestrial or animal-vegetative; the two upper lines are heavenly or spiritual; and the two middle lines represent man and his soul. Hence there is Heaven and Earth — the two poles of Existence — with Man as connecting link; or spirit and matter, and in this case living matter, as the two poles of human existence, and the soul as tie.

K'an (water) and Li (fire) unite in 63 AFTER COMPLETION and 64 BEFORE COMPLETION,

It is 63 AFTER COMPLETION which represents union for all three, Earth, Man and Heaven, because the couplets of each move towards each other. But there is a tendency to a separation *between* Earth, Man and Heaven. In 64 BEFORE COMPLETION there is a tendency to separation *within* Earth, Man and Heaven, but there is unification *between* them.

When Chen (thunder) and Ken (mountain) unite in 53 DEVELOPMENT and 18 DECAY

both situations are united in the middle lines representing Man, but in 53 DEVELOPMENT, Heaven and Earth emphasize their own yang and yin tendency. Man here must unify Heaven and Earth within himself which is a gradual development. Earth is all yin according to its nature; and Heaven is all yang according to its nature. Man is the changing line in the golden hexagram interpretation and being a 6 = —×— = is integrative rather than separative.

In 18 WORK ON DECAY Heaven and Earth tend towards separations within themselves and Man is the integrator. This implies work in both body and spirit through the psyche. Earth is a repetition of Heaven, but each are divided within themselves.

When Chen (thunder) and Tui (lake) are combined we get either 54 THE MARRYING MAID or 17 FOLLOWING

In 54 MARRYING MAID, Earth is in Heaven and Heaven in Earth which creates a great attraction; but the middle lines are not in accord and tend to separate. Man here is not integral and this creates a dangerous situation.

In 17 FOLLOWING, the fifth line is yang and the second line is yin which is suited to their places (the opposite is the case with 54 THE MARRYING MAID). In FOLLOWING this creates a favorable situation as long as Man in the middle is adaptable. Heaven and Earth are united in themselves and Man has to adapt to their model.

TRIGRAMS AS 'INNER' AND 'OUTER'

Another rule as a clue of interpretation is in understanding the qualities of the trigrams as elements and getting a 'feeling' for correspondences. Then interpret the lower trigram as the inner aspect.

You can imagine the inner aspect as embodied within you (Earth). The upper trigram is the outer aspect. You can imagine it as extended from you as aspirations (Heaven).

For example, in 44 ENCOUNTERING ☰☴ Heaven is above the wind, Creative above Penetrating:

Here one is embodying the penetrating and gentle quality of wind and projecting aspirations of Heaven. Since Heaven is here already full (all yang lines), the yin line from below, tending downward, creates sexual connotations of temptation. One's aspirations are yang, but the dark yin line entering the body from below tends to separate from one's aspirations. Thus there is a dark principle hidden in the body which is not in harmony with one's aspirations.

24 RETURN ☷☳ the opposite hexagram to 44 ENCOUNTERING, shows a yang line entering the situation. It tends to rise upward into open receptive aspirations. This new positive energy tends to increase the yang even though there is only one yang line in the whole hexagram. One's aspirations are spacious and open, ready to receive the rising energy.

The hexagrams which are mirror images of 44 ENCOUNTERING and 24 RETURN are 43 RESOLUTION ☱☰ and 23 SPLITTING APART ☶☷

They are opposites of each other, as are 44 ENCOUNTER-

ING and 24 RETURN.

In 23 SPLITTING APART the top yang line is rising and separating from the yin lines of the upper trigram of aspirations. There is an embodiment of the receptive principle, but the outer situation is dividing. Although the inner situation is open and receptive, there is nothing to receive. Instead, this hexagram suggests a time of releasing, dying to be reborn and ceasing to cling to any expectations. This is a time to prepare for complete vacuity.

In 43 RESOLUTION, on the contrary, the top yin line tends to sink and provides a receptacle to the expansive yang aspirations. There is a full embodiment of yang energy inwardly which tends to rise up towards great power. It is a time to make resolves, decisions and affirm the full qualities of life.

THE WISDOM OF BODY-PSYCHE-SPIRIT

Since, according to Wilhelm, there is a correspondence of Earth and body, Man and psyche or soul, and Heaven or spirit, we can see that the hexagrams reveal these triple interfaces, all of which are changing. Awareness always shines, but intuition opens the door to let the light in. Inner and outer are aspects of Man embodying and aspiring towards unity, the Integral Harmonious body.

Experiences are sometimes born of karma which is a deposit of body, psyche and spirit patterns. These are our circumstances, but our intuition brings us to an awareness which is free of circumstances. By awareness of body, psyche and spirit continuously changing, we can develop character. With character we can shape our life. Character is our essence brought out from circumstances like metal, fired by the heat of love, fused with wisdom, and cast into the mould of integrity.

The hexagrams are to be intuitively witnessed, not identified with. The mind projects, imagines and the body is a memory deposit of 'past' experiences. In truth, there is no future and no past, but only this integral present awareness which includes all moments. Awareness is timeless.

As with anything, the greatest danger of the oracle is if we become bound by a particular hexagram which we interpret as either good or evil, which then affirms our fear or desire. But this is not the *I Ching*'s fault! It has no control over what anyone thinks, fears or imagines anymore than other people do. We can only free ourselves from such attachments and aversions by an attentive serene mind. If it is agitated, then it is best to be quiet and accepting until it becomes quiet also.

Unnecessary fear and desire bring suffering and then blame is put on others. It is harder to put the blame on the *I Ching* because it is neutral. It says what the present situation is and gives counsel. It in no way coerces anyone to think, be or do anything whatsoever.

GOLDEN HEXAGRAM SPECTRUMS OF INTERPRETATION

Another way to interpret is suggested in Commentary 5 on the three levels of polarities of the golden hexagrams. Not only are we then realizing that the bottom two lines relate to our body, the middle two lines to our psyche and the top two lines to our spirit, but there is a scale of attachment and detachment by which to assess our relation with the hexagram.

This is a means by which to evaluate whether you are angry or fearful, hurt or full of desires through your body, which become manifest in physical sensations. This is a way to realizing the vast spectrum of levels to interpret the *same* hexagram at different times.

If your psyche is disturbed (middle two lines) then look at whether it is on the basis of delusion or imagination (if the line is yang), repression or remembering (if the line is yin). The spectrum of unconsciousness and conscious awareness is great and you can evaluate the level of integration they have within you at any moment.

This implies that if you draw the same hexagram later on, you will have a different interpretation because of the change in your own state of consciousness. You can witness this yourself by watching your mind and internal imagery. If you have a calm mind (either active or passive) you can see things as they are, but if the mind jumps about and polarizes in conflict, then look at whether the third and fourth lines of the hexagram you've drawn are yin or yang and try to get to the root of the problem. The oracle is a kind of detective. It helps you spot the source of anxieties. Awareness alone begins a process of bringing the gross delusions and separative stages of the spectrum into integral, subtle and clear insight.

Again, the spirit, represented by the top two lines, has a spectrum from great separation of ego and objects-others to great compassion and wisdom.

With the spirit you evaluate your aspirations and whether they include or exclude others. If your aspirations tend to separate and reject rather than encompass and develop empathy for others, then get to the root quality of the yin or yang lines. This will manifest in you as spiritual anxieties or a sense of invulnerable, fearless confidence.

Physical pain (bottom lines) is difficult, but spiritual anxiety (top lines) is even harder because one cannot easily locate the source of the problem. This is not done by exchanging goals or ideals, but in practising moving *towards* rather than *away from* one's anxieties. By merging with the problem, one comes into a unitive state; whereas avoidance brings greater separation, a sense of self-importance, anxiety and tension. If the top lines are yang, allow spiritual suffering to turn to compassion. If the top lines are yin, allow your sense of alienation to become united in the wisdom of knowing others as yourself.

Desires are not the root of the problem, but attachment to desires is. Such attachment divides us against ourselves and consequently from others. Desires are ways to expand one's awareness, ways of being one with everything. If we attach to them, it is worse than if they were never brought to our attention.

Life itself brings desire, but desire is not an ultimate source. Desire is natural when it is in harmony with one's being. Life is a stream of continuous changes from the Tao and immeasurable are its qualities. It is only ego-attachment that distorts desire and interprets qualities as 'good' and 'evil'. From the one being of Wu Chi, to the polarity of T'ai Chi and the four-fold pattern, through the eight trigrams and the sixty-four hexagrams and 384 changing lines, and the thousands of permutations, we have orders of qualities which are the beauty of the universe.

These orders of the flow of life can help us understand the wholeness of our lives in harmony with life itself. In this way there is no absolute separation, but there are appreciations of the different qualities and orders which give life its interest.

We have all these qualities and cycles within ourselves. If we didn't, how could we recognize them in the 'world'? The separation of the self and the world is a projection of the mind. When we assume responsibility for how we see the world, we can live at peace with it, for it is within ourselves.

Projecting everything outward from the mind is an escape from fear of the undesirable or a search from desire of the desirable. When our deepest being accepts both what we desire and what we fear, unfounded fears and desires cease.

We cannot escape from what we fear, for all obsessions follow us everywhere. We can only stop feeding them, spending energy propping them up and nursing them.

We cannot bargain with the oracle or cheat it into giving us something we are unworthy of. Life gives us opportunities to respond and be, as well as a body-psyche-spirit with which to respond and be, and the oracle reveals a holistic pattern for us. What more can we ask? What we are and do with it is up to us.

TIGER AND DRAGON INTERPRETATIONS

Finally, we can interpret the hexagrams according to the qualities of the Tiger and Dragon, relating this to the masculine and feminine subtle currents as in Taoist Yoga (see Commentary 7). This is the basis of the judgments given in this book. When you read the oracle given in this book, allow it to penetrate to your unconscious mind and trust your first intuitions.

The oracle is a book of wisdom and with love we can take this wisdom into ourselves. Everything but our love and wisdom can be stolen, lost or can decay or be destroyed. The changes are temporary, the momentary states continuously change, but the wisdom we glean from the changes is changeless and indestructible. Fears and desires are temporary, but the true love-will which embraces both is changeless. Thus the true Self is invulnerable.

CREATIVITY AND INTUITION

These methods of interpretation are given as examples of how to apply intuition to rules. Intuition is spontaneous because it springs up in the present living moment. Intuition comes from the timeless and is irresistible if we accept the truth. The oracle reflects the spontaneous present on the mirror of the psyche. Whether we can read it or not depends on our intuition.

The oracle itself is a mirror, very sensitive to the subtlest cosmic vibrations and to the tiny particular patterns of our immediate lives. It is timeless as wisdom is timeless. It does not show us a whole film at any one moment, but only a tiny frame, an instant: the present situation, that is, the situation of inquiry. And this it reflects very deeply in myriads of ways.

Intuitive seeing is more than sensory seeing, for the whole being embraces reality and is simultaneously embraced by it. 'If thine eye be single, thy whole body will be full of light.'

When intuition is open, creativity manifests far beyond the apparent capacities of the individual. For the whole flow of the universal order is spontaneously behind the truly pure and intuitive act. The oracle is a way of totality (*wholeness*) which is simultaneously very specific (specific lines of hexagrams); and he who uses it intuitively can 'tune in' to the magnitude of the *whole*.

That everything in life is changing we are all witnesses to. But there is an eternal reality behind the changes. It is the changeless which is to be revealed through the changes.

These suggestions for interpretation are a dialogue with the reader's self about change in order to experience reality directly. It is advised therefore to never become attached to words, images, diagrams or any aspect of the changes as if they were anything in themselves. They are passages; open doorways through which to pass.

When a person is *one* with his/her true Self, reality, a person is *one* with all things. Then everything a person does or doesn't do is naturally harmonious. The changes are like the flow of water — from clouds and rain to streamlets, waterfalls, underground passages, rivers, torrents, fountains, geysers and the rising in plant stems, eddies and rivulets, all the way to the great sea. All is life. There is no death anywhere. Therefore reality is the changes and yet is eternal.

When intuitively attuning to the hexagram you have drawn from the oracle, you do well to 'feel' the subtle qualities in it and keep a calm, neutral attitude. There is a lucid resonance between our present state at any one moment and the hexagram drawn.

As an analogy, when we look at the water with turbulent waves in our minds, we cannot see the mountain and the sky reflected in it. The hexagrams represent various degrees of subtle qualities and the more serene our minds, the more we can see into these qualities. We need to empty our minds of past memories and imaginings until, with mind and body quiet, we see the clarity of the situation. When awareness shines we cannot identify with either the water or the image reflected in it.

— 3 —
How to read the individual lines

When using the coin, stick or seed method, you may have changing lines. The changing lines are specific, whereas the hexagram as a whole is general. The changing lines are 6 = −×− or 9 = −○−. When you have drawn one or more changing lines, the procedure is to look up both hexagrams from the key.

In the seed method, you will have only one changing line, resulting from your count of the seventh pile of seeds.

In the coin or stalk method,

when a line is a 6 −×−, yin − − changes to yang −−−−
when a line is a 9 −○−, yang −−−− changes to yin − −

Consequently:

<table>
<tr><td></td><td>first
hexagram</td><td></td><td>second
hexagram</td></tr>
<tr><td> is</td><td></td><td>changing to</td><td></td></tr>
<tr><td></td><td>35 PROGRESS</td><td></td><td>42 INCREASE</td></tr>
</table>

Except when all the lines are changing, always read only the lines which change from the *first* hexagram.

The changing lines indicate specific attitudes or situations and in general overrule or have priority even over the hexagram as a whole if there is a conflict of meaning or directives. The changing line indicates specific attitudes or conditions inherent in the present situation and the hexagram changed into indicates the direction of transformation.

In general, the following rules apply to priorities in interpretation of lines (not applicable to the seed method where only one line changing is possible):

32

1 When one line is changing, this is very significant and should be read.

2 When two lines are changing and both are 9s —○— or both are 6s —×— read the top line as priority over the lower line.

3 In the stick (or stalk) method only, when two lines are changing and one is a 6 —×— and one is a 9 —○—, take the 6 —×— as priority regardless of whether it is the upper or lower line.

4 When you have three changing lines, give priority to the middle line.

5 When you have drawn four changing lines, use the *upper non-changing* line for interpretation.

6 When you have drawn five changing lines, use the *non-changing* line for interpretation.

7 When all six lines are changing, *use the second hexagram as more significant in your interpretation* than the first hexagram. In the case of 1 the CREATIVE or 2 the RECEPTIVE read the interpretation of all changing lines given at the end of the lines of those hexagrams.

The lines represent time from below upward. The duration of time to be interpreted depends on the time frame of your question. If the time period is a year, then each line represents two months; if a month, then each line represents five days. If your question involves the time period of a week, then each line represents a day and in the seventh day the outcome will be realized. If your question involves only a day, then each line is equal to four hours; if the immediate hour is the question, then each line amounts to only ten minutes.

Reading from below upwards the first, third and fifth lines are odd numbered and are most beneficially yang. Sometimes a yin line in these places is beneficial. This is an exceptional case, such as a yin line amongst five yang lines in 14 POSSESSION IN GREAT MEASURE.

The second, fourth and sixth lines are even numbered and are most beneficially yin. Only exceptionally is a yang line beneficial in even numbered places, as in 8 UNITY, 16 ENTHUSIASM OR 7 The ARMY when all the other lines are yin.

The lines of a hexagram have correspondences and affinities with each other. The first two lines have affinity as 'Earth' or the body. The third and fourth lines have affinity as 'Man' or the psyche; and the fifth and sixth lines have affinity as 'Heaven' or the spirit. It is beneficial if there is both a yin and yang line in each of these three levels.

Another level of beneficial correspondence is to have paired yin and yang lines in relation to the upper and lower trigrams. Then the bottom line has affinity with the fourth line, the second line with the fifth and the third line with the sixth. Generally it is beneficial to have a yang line in the bottom line when the fourth line is yin.

— 4 —
Change, chance and synchronicity

Change is conquered by *awareness* of change. In the continuous instants which stream forth from the creation of each moment, we realize the eternal now. Instants are images which become aware of themselves in the simultaneous. Each instant is a creative T'ai Chi and a monadic whole without sequence which, like a cell of a hologram, contains the image of the whole hologram.

In this awareness, there is no cause but a continuous mutual arising of constellations of energy. The infinite points of instants through space have no 'before' and no 'after', for they live in an imaginal reality where time as sequence does not arise.

Every instant is a whole, containing the pattern of both instants and golden images. Each mind-moment is continuously creating all universes. Past and future are contained in each present. Causality is polar, not sequential. The pole of creation arises simultaneously with the pole of awareness, of quality, image and meaning.

In this view, causes are not separate from events, but are mirrors of them. You cannot trace it to a final cause because the law of correspondences, by which an event and its meaning arise, is not linear. C. G. Jung calls it synchronicity.

Synchronicity is a cosmic ecology wherein every mind-moment is the whole, a simultaneous arising of mind and matter, image and substance. It is nothing and in its nothingness *being is*. Time is created by the psyche (read psyche as mind and soul combined) to realize 'heaven' in 'earth' and 'earth' in 'heaven'. The immortality of the psyche is in being aware instant by instant of the whole and being true to oneself. Through change is realized the unchanging.

Karma, or past deposits of tendencies, is continuously disappearing and reappearing each instant. These deposits are recorded as the changing and unchanging triple lines of the golden hexagrams. Through the truth of the wholeness of each instant, comes the possibility of freedom from past tendencies (conditions and circumstances) and future expectations (projection of past tendencies).

Our bodies are flame-like in their golden essences continuously flowing, dynamic, alive. The husks of our imaginal bodies or souls go through a recycling in birth, childhood, maturity, old age and death, while the awareness of the psyche continues by each instant afresh and growing in awareness.

Nothing could be more valuable for becoming aware of each whole instant than the practice of a book of wisdom like the *I Ching*. Each golden hexagram of the Tiger and Dragon Oracle is a constellation of the present aura of the questioner. Our life (what the Taoists call immortality) is in the continuous creativity of each instant being awake.

From this understanding, we are not a combination of body and spirit as the classical Aristotelian view would have it. Spiritualism and materialism divided from each other are both diseases of our culture. It is like 'Heaven' and 'Earth' without 'Man' as the proper mediating principle of wisdom and compassion. Both spirit and body bind and condition the psyche which is the mediator. To free the bondage is to realize the mutual arising of body and spirit in image and meaning. This is creative life, simultaneously arising anew without past debris of the conditioned mind in a trail of time. The golden hexagrams are a mirror of each state of newness.

Like an artist, we can create our lives anew. The subtle body of the soul emanates through the aura by which the divination methods receive a constellation, at once duplicating the subatomic instantaneous level and the imaginal or virtual level of reality. The quantitative is realized through the qualitative. Pure spontaneity is free of conditions and free of time. *It is not doing what we want, but wanting what spontaneous creativity does through us.*

Divinity or Tao is dispersed in matter and to become integral beings is to regather what has been scattered throughout the universe. We can recognize ourselves thereby, in the smallest beings and events, by the law of correspondences.

The golden hexagrams can be used to realize ourselves as integral beings, not merely to get answers to our anxieties. The dismemberment of the 'god' is to be reunited by each one of us realizing the 'I am' of each instant, each stone, plant and person through the awakening of the creative psyche.

By becoming aware of the etheric currents throughout the body, the Dragon is reunited with the Tiger and the circulation of the subtle Ch'i brings one in resonance with the whole universe and the wholeness of the Universal Mind.

In this way the eternal is realized in time, the simultaneous is known in the instant, and the spirit is realized in the body through the psyche. In a sense, the Tiger consumes time, as the INNER TRUTH of the red tongues of flame. The Tiger, like suns, is generated by the vibratory awakening of Logos (to use Greek terms) in Eros.

And the Dragon consumes space as he is the abysmal void and Humble Vigilance of being nothing. The Dragon, like the vast darkness of space, is the vital waters and nerve plexus which is the vibratory desire of Eros in Logos.

The Dragon as Eros in Logos changes from the APPROACH of the arousing thunderous quality to the still CONTEM-PLATIVE quality of the mountain. Clouds and mist circle the mountain-tops where the Dragon dwells. He sends his vibrations down like rain and streams to fertilize the land.

The Tiger as Logos in Eros changes from the RETREAT of the penetrating gaze and invisible wind into the POWER OF THE GREAT of the clear reflective lake. The Tiger leaves no trace and hides herself lest all animals flee from her. Yet she drives all bodies into action from primary desire and she aids in sublimating the desire into the pure love of the heart by being both silent and great. May you find the Tiger and Dragon within you through this oracle.

PART II

The sixty-four Golden Hexagrams of the Tiger and Dragon Oracle

Introduction

If you are using coins or yarrow stalks, then look up the appropriate hexagram from the key at the end of the book combining trigrams and consult the following text. If you are using cards, then consult the following text directly, according to the number on the card you have drawn.

In the following text there are five aspects to consider:

1 The IMAGE (picture) and corresponding poetic statement of Tiger and Dragon currents for *intuitive* interpretation.
2 The MOON-CYCLES according to a binary arrangement of the hexagrams (see Commentary 8) which can suggest either outward actions (earthly view) or inner insights (heavenly view).
3 The JUDGMENT which gives the tendency of the situation and gives counsel on attitudes or actions suitable with respect to your question. 'Feel out' whether its counsel seems true or not and do as you will.
4 MAN or WOMAN special readings which give more specific counsel according to the sex of the questioner. In a few cases there is no difference of reading for the two sexes, but most give complementary suggestions.
5 The LINES which are relevant when changing, when using coins or yarrow stalks. The lines are shown with their changing line forms of 6 = —×— and 9 = —○—. If you cast a changing hexagram, read only the applicable lines of the *first* hexagram, not the hexagram it changes into.

1 CREATIVE

THE IMAGE

Rainbow Jewels Vaporize into White Light

The Tiger and Dragon spring from the head of the pure
   white light of HEAVEN.
Being and non-being are not separate and freedom flows
   from the creative action of heaven moving within the
   receptive earth. Fullness and emptiness, action and non-
   action proceed from quiescence.

HEAVENLY MOON CYCLE

The CREATIVE is the truly invisible and spiritual light free of moon cycles as time. It is the final reflection of light on light through the positive subtle currents. The pivot point of the whole moon cycle is the beginning of a return by polarity to the RECEPTIVE. Binary 63.

JUDGMENT

The CREATIVE is the dynamic yang principle at its peak wherein the copulation of the Dragon and Tiger takes place.

This is a time of powerful inspiration, energy and fulfillment. The cosmic order is in complete accord with your motivations and actions. It is time to rid yourself of anything irrelevant to your most strong destiny.

Abundant creativity is within you now and if you move forth spontaneously without conceptualizing too much, you will realize your creative power. Now is a good time to be active and to take initiative. Feel the fire or light in your heart and allow your spiritual value to express itself in harmony with the Tao.

Yin and yang are like two wings and you need them both, but now is a yang time for you. Use it well as an expression of the highest spiritual creative energy. You can do things now that you would previously have struggled with. Have confidence and direct your creative powers into righteous channels.

MAN

For a man, now is a time wherein inspiration and ideas for the creative advancement of humanity are born. Righteous ideals will be successful. At this time you can be your most creative self without any inhibitions. Keep the highest aims of your community in mind and act with sagacious intuition.

WOMAN

For a woman, this is a time wherein full creative manifestation is possible. This may be a pregnancy of some kind but not necessarily children. It is a time where a woman can bring her power of creativity into dynamic activity. A sense of timing of when and how to take action is important. At this time, a woman will know the wisdom of this by being in accord with the creative flow of the cosmos.

LINES

6 Your cup will be emptied soon. Realize how to retreat as well as advance. Extreme creativity leads to decline.

5 By resonance, like attracts like. Your virtue attracts others of similar qualities with whom you can work.

4 This is a test. Follow your intuition as to whether to advance or retreat. You will know how to adapt harmoniously to the situation.

3 Continue working on virtue and character. Then integrity will be yours and all things can be accomplished.

2 If your highest aspirations resonate with one you have met, contribute your gifts of virtue to his or her purpose.

1 Do not compromise yourself for the time is not yet come to exercise your true power and virtue. Have patience.

All changing lines: your comprehension and virtue are great enough to encompass the entire cosmos! Excellent creative action.

▤ 2 RECEPTIVE ▤

THE IMAGE

Vast Seas of Caves and Valleys Condense into Coals of Fire

The belly of the dark EARTH opens passage to receive both Tiger and Dragon in a profound union.

The cave of the earth is the mother's devotion of receiving without discrimination. Her vast space absorbs and transmutes all mixtures of good and ill. Listen and all will be transformed.

EARTHLY MOON CYCLE

The RECEPTIVE is the complete yin state of receptivity preceding the moon cycle. It is self-reflecting and all-absorbing. Binary 0.

JUDGMENT

The RECEPTIVE is the open yin principle wherein the copulation of the Tiger and Dragon results in the prominence of the feminine principle.

Now is a time to fully realize the harvest of your life and also to empty yourself of extraneous projects and pursuits. Respond and follow the leadership of those enlightened. Examine the succession of the phases of your life and siphon out from it those aspects of greatest virtue. Persist in those virtuous qualities with great devotion and release anything that hinders them.

You may align yourself with someone who is a leader or you may find that leader within yourself. For now, accept the darkness around you and move through it with faith. Then great accomplishments will be yours. Don't attempt to do everything yourself, but delegate appropriate tasks. Strength now lies in accepting your own weaknesses and being responsive rather than initiating.

WOMAN

For a woman, the RECEPTIVE is a time of mystery, of the unknown, but also of great intuition. This is a peak time of subtle awareness of the 'luminous darkness'. Be serene amidst confusion and a new order will be received. Respond to others spontaneously, according to good-will, and a joy will well up in your heart.

Accept your weakness just now and strength will come from a higher order. Don't attempt to do anything yourself but respond to everything. This means emptiness of will and fullness of the earth. This is body and abundance by natural accord with the fruition of life. The ripening of fruit takes care of itself if you serve by watering and fertilizing. Nothing need be done except plucking the fruit.

Tune in to what the earth as a whole needs. Regard it as the living being that it is and listen to its distress. Respond in any way you can.

MAN

For a man, the RECEPTIVE is a time of lowered energies. This may mean sexual arousal and if so, it is well to do nothing, but allow the energies to be absorbed throughout the body.

Spend some time alone and remain open to intuitive and subtle insights concerning your life and destiny. You will find new guidance by releasing old thought patterns and habits and realizing vast spacious potentials within you. First it is necessary to go beyond the temptations of clinging to old pleasures and thoughts, not by repression, but by quiet witnessing.

LINES

—x—   6 An aggressive and willful attempt to gain power results in struggle and the result is exhaustion of being. Competition destroys where cooperation harmonizes.

—x—   5 It is well to allow virtue to permeate your life without display. Your inner worth is all that is needed. Your own receptive centering harmonizes others.

—x—   4 Be cautious, taciturn and calm. Keep a low profile and be vigilant and receptive to good advice or insights.

—x—   3 Keep your reserves hidden and keep yourself docile and all things will come to fruition without effort. Humble service in daily life is beneficial.

—x—   2 Work only on your inner awareness and intuition. Whatever you do will go well as long as you do nothing! What is well planted grows by itself.

—x—   1 All that you are is an accumulation of your past and if you have piled up virtues, all will go well. New tasks require a gentle, receptive, open mind aware of your own past mistakes.

All changing lines: endure all things to the end and by maintaining your awareness throughout all that comes to you, good fortune.

3 DIFFICULTY AT BEGINNING

THE IMAGE

Vast Seas of Jewels Condense into Lightning

The belly of the dark EARTH receives and yields to the FIRES of life through the eyes of the Tiger.

In DIFFICULTY movements in advancing cannot be lightly undertaken. Untie the knots of destiny and weave new fabrics of lasting value.

EARTHLY MOON CYCLE

Just after full moon is a time to consolidate and reflect on what has been accomplished. Difficulties in active life lead to insights. Binary 17.

JUDGMENT

DIFFICULTY is the transformation of the RECEPTIVE feminine principle into the INNER TRUTH OF THE TIGER.

This is a time of new birth as if from the void of the receptive principle where inevitably there are unknowns and seeming chaos. The maelstrom of activity may be difficult, but by great activity in harmonious directions things will be put in order. Just work on what is at hand.

The apparent confusion is actually a creative matrix, but it is not a time to willfully take action. Rather, one must be receptive, patient and open to find the INNER TRUTH of the situation within one's heart.

MAN

For a man, this means that the subtle current moves from the sexual center directly into the heart. This is such a short circuit that the profusion of energy does not find easy awareness until it comes into the heart. Rather it may seem hopeless just when it is not.

Above all, it is not a time to force the issue or allow passion to run rampant. The energy can flow upward into the heart without pushing. One must maintain an open attitude of honesty to realize what and how the situation is to be born.

WOMAN

For a woman, the subtle current moves from the head down to the sexual center and into the heart. The struggle for new birth for the woman is that of intuition and open receptivity to insights and guidance.

It is not a literal birth so much as a formative time of the deep Self. It is wise to be open to guidance both within and without. As difficulties press upon one, it is advisable to not resist or struggle, but accept help and to distribute the load so that a more calm atmosphere can prevail whereby the INNER TRUTH is known in the heart and the difficulties removed.

LINES

—x— 6 Your difficulties can only be solved by becoming detached from what concerns you. Begin again.

—o— 5 Attempt only small projects, not large ones; for you have inner authority even though it is not yet established outwardly. Don't push.

—x— 4 You need help and by accepting it you will fulfill your goals. You may feel hesitant but good fortune awaits you.

—x— 3 If you are wise you will be calm and not plunge into activity now. There is an impasse before you and it is best to give up your desires now.

—x— 2 Don't attempt to make decisions now. Let life come and go as it will. It may be difficult but understanding will be reached.

—o— 1 Keep your highest vision and maintain integrity, but don't attempt to push ahead now. Unite with others of similar situation.

4 IMMATURITY

THE IMAGE

Vast Seas of Mountains Consense into Comets and Stars

The eye of the baby Tiger sees the FLAMES of truth changing into the obscurity of the belly of the dark EARTH.

IMMATURITY is that state of alchemical work wherein the immortal foetus is conceived. This is a fragile time and not a time to pull up roots or ask too many questions. Move forward.

HEAVENLY MOON CYCLE

The moon elixir in the deep unconsciousness is surfacing to the conscious mind. Danger and even folly is a necessary process in the unfoldment of wisdom. Binary 34.

JUDGMENT

IMMATURITY is the transformation of the INNER TRUTH OF THE TIGER into the RECEPTIVE UNION OF THE TIGER AND DRAGON.

At this time unless there is a sincere desire for the truth and receptivity when it comes, there will be confusion and perplexity. Confusion in itself is harmless unless it spreads itself by repeated useless questions without wanting to know the answers. Therefore sincere desire for truth is the necessary initial state of consciousness needed now.

You are inexperienced in the matter at hand and this is an opportunity to gain experience in untrod territory. To do so means the likelihood of making mistakes and falling into confusion from time to time. Do not be troubled by your naivety in this, but flow on with as much decisiveness as you can. Persist in your thoroughness to experience as many aspects of the situation as possible. Then you will receive teachings of invaluable importance.

WOMAN

For a woman, IMMATURITY is a sincere quest which must be brought into a meditative discipline whereby clarity will be born of intuition. If, however, too much will is applied, you may overshoot the mark and not be open to disciplining the body and mind to being receptive. Then your genuine search will go through many phases of question and answer before your own intuitive realization is born.

Cultivate your own character through a deep probing of what matters most to you in your life. If you can focus all your questions into one big question, the true teacher will be found. Whether this is another person or your own inner voice or guidance is up to cosmic circumstances. The main thing is to continue in one direction of search for your most comprehensive questions.

MAN

For a man, IMMATURITY is a time wherein the heart of the matter must be examined and brought to bear in a complete circuit of changes before you can become calm enough to learn what is happening. Don't be impatient, but continue in posing questions which come from the heart of the matter. If you ask irrelevant questions at this time you will not be able to keep your head above the confusion.

If you wait and probe before posing a clear question to either yourself or a guide and teacher, you will be able to move into very creative processes which will bring you to an increased awareness of what you are experiencing. Be then receptive and open to truly learning from experience.

LINES

—o— 6 Punishment is natural as a way to realize where you have gone wrong. Accept it and further wrongs will be prevented.

—x— 5 Innocence is rewarded even when foolish, for the young, soft and fragile states are always vulnerable.

—x— 4 Don't be stubborn now or it will lead to humiliation. Be flexible and open to learning.

—x— 3 Cease trying to hold on to what you desire, for your energies are wasted in possessiveness.

—o— 2 Being compassionate and gentle with the young is very beneficial. This will eventually lead to their cultivation and in any case there is good in this.

—x— 1 Certainly discipline or guidelines are needed, but nothing rash. The appropriate measure of rules can be made.

THE IMAGE

Relfecting Sands Penetrate into White Light

The feet of the Dragon run on THUNDER discharging energy into the pure white light of HEAVEN.

The egg stage of metamorphosis is the incubation of letting the creative idea emerge of its own accord in its own time. The egg is the means by which life comes into being through WAITING.

EARTHLY MOON CYCLE

Just before waning half moon there is not much to be done but enjoy the moment. See friends and live in the present. Binary 23.

JUDGMENT

In WAITING we see the APPROACH OF THE DRAGON changing into the COPULATION OF THE TIGER AND DRAGON in the CREATIVE. It is not yet a time to express your full creative powers. Rather, the energy is building with great abundance from within.

There may be some anxiety as the Dragon approaches and as the energy currents mount, but this is a time to just live in the present and throw away all ifs and buts. The present is full of the flow of the Tao, and you need only to wait, enjoying the rising energy.

You have a distinct possibility of reaching your aims if you don't get too impatient. Eventually there will be celebration, but meanwhile calm down and nullify all radical behaviour. Expectation and anxiety bring only reckless destruction of all you have worked for and aspire to. Remain sincere in your intent and difficulties will be overcome.

The ability to wait is powerful, for if you can wait, others will have confidence in you. Perform ordinary actions in daily life to the best of your ability and all will be well.

MAN

For a man, now is a time of great flow of positive energy and you should have confidence that all will be well though it is not a time to act. Rather, waiting is just what it says: wait with certainty of creative energy ascending.

WOMAN

For a woman, WAITING is a time of inner vision and waiting with awareness of the present situation. It is the descending current from the 'Inner Eye' down to the sexual center. It is not time to act or to manifest yet. Rather, allow the vision to go deeper into the imaginal realm where subtle energy fields mount.

Certainly it is not a time for release of energy, either in sexual encounters, or in large activities. It is a time of allowing energy to increase in vision and awareness so that clarity is present when it is time to manifest action.

LINES

-x- 6 Danger. It seems impossible, but three events which you may not recognize are relevant will help you out of the present danger.

-o- 5 Relax through ordinary pleasures such as eating and drinking in moderation. Keep vigilant.

-x- 4 Chaos and confusion. Do nothing that would entangle you further in the situation and you will be free of it.

-o- 3 Be cautious for danger is all around you. By vigilance and a calm mind you can stay free of unnecessary difficulty.

-o- 2 Don't attempt to forge ahead now for others will not understand and the time is not ripe for action. Patience.

-o- 1 Remain a witness of the situation and keep a constant heart. Maintain attentive serenity and low profile.

6 CONFLICT

THE IMAGE

Streaming Jewels Explode into Comets and Stars

The head of the white light of HEAVEN shines down on the conflict of the hands of the Dragons beneath the MOUNTAIN.

The caterpillar hatches out of the egg and the newly born have great desires and fears. Do not eat everything in your path. The beginning of consumption meets with CONFLICT.

HEAVENLY MOON CYCLE

The danger now is between the way of Heaven which tends to rise and the abysmal waters which tend to sink. The conflict arises from the radiance of the moon elixir in the depths of one's being while the unconscious mind still resists the dissolving of the false ego. Binary 58.

JUDGMENT

CONFLICT is the CREATIVE UNION OF THE TIGER AND DRAGON changing into the CONTEMPLATION OF THE DRAGON.

Direct opposition leads one now to contemplate. There is no way to circumvent the conflict by putting it off or going around it. You can only stop and go within and contemplate the source of the present conflict.

You have a great deal of creative energy now, but it is wise to reconsider how to use this energy. If used aggressively in home, work or politics, it will reveal the conflict immediately. If there are misunderstandings, go back to the beginning and inquire into your own motives. Ask an impartial observer and consider the cause of the obstacles in your life now. Get to the root of the problem by being as neutral as possible and asking how the two opposing points of view came about. Let your creative energy enter into contemplation of the source of the issue rather than what you want.

WOMAN

For a woman, CONFLICT is a time of great unconscious arousal which could be very destructive if not brought up into consciousness. Open confrontations are very dangerous at this time. Your powerfully aroused energy cannot cease, but it can be directed into channels which lead you to greater insight about the source of the present conflict.

At first it is beneficial to focus your mind on some landscape or place of beauty which calms you. Instead of fixating on the conflict at hand, use conscious effort to bring yourself to a state of equanimity. This will enable you to understand your opponent better and receive an overview enabling the conflict to be resolved.

Do not try to bring your projects or points of view into fruition, but stand back, ask what is right and accept what your deepest contemplation brings.

MAN

For a man, CONFLICT is the change of energy from inspiration and ideas to a more 'letting be' attitude. It is a time to allow insights to come spontaneously rather than making an effort to push through ideas. Relinquish your position if it is rigid, but hold to it quietly if it is right. Above all, do not become cunning or clever in designing strategies to overcome the opposition. Rather, restore your energy by allowing your anxieties to dissolve. This will bring an impartial and fruitful contemplation.

LINES

—o— 6 By using force, you can win the immediate conflict, but such action will rebound on you and the repercussions will give you no peace of mind.

—o— 5 In the present conflict, it is beneficial to find a just mediator and allow righteousness to be discovered.

—o— 4 Although you are stronger than your opponent, do not attempt to win the conflict now. There is no inner value to overcoming the other. Return to peace.

—x— 3 Affirm your inner worth and do not be concerned with advancements. Prominence now is to be avoided and true values will be eventually established.

—o— 2 Retreat from the conflict, for your adversary is now stronger than you. Those close to you will not suffer if you withdraw.

—x— 1 Even if you have been a victim, forgive and pass on. Terminate any dispute quickly and all will be well.

7 THE ARMY

THE IMAGE

Vast Seas of Caves and Valleys Condense into Comets and Stars

The feet of the Dragon electrify clouds of THUNDER for the resources in the belly of the dark EARTH.

The multitudes are in firmness, held together by need. The embryonic consciousness consolidates in the womb and the watery spring nourishes the power of the leader.

EARTHLY MOON CYCLE

As energy increases, more discipline is needed. There is danger from the power of the rising moon elixir currents unless held in control by the wisdom of timing. Binary 2.

JUDGMENT

THE ARMY is the APPROACH OF THE DRAGON changing into the RECEPTIVE UNION OF THE TIGER AND DRAGON.

Reserves of energy are gathered together now and great discipline is needed to master it. It is dangerous to have great storage of powerful forces unless strict obedience to a wise leader takes place.

Your approach to the situation demands that either you are in command or that you follow. Do not hesitate to take charge if this is your calling. If so, then persist in both giving instruction and disciplining those subordinate to you. Do not wield authority ruthlessly. Rather be generous with noble-hearted awareness of what is best for all concerned.

The community, nation or world as a whole must be considered now. Then you will be given the communal support of forces. These decisions concern all of humanity and the war to be waged is with malevolence and unruly thoughts and deeds.

If instead, you are a follower, adapt to the needs of the organization at this time so that the group as a whole can benefit. This does not mean giving up your values but persisting in serving them by pledging yourself to help if need arises. Meanwhile cultivate justice while dealing with those around you.

WOMAN

For a woman, THE ARMY is a time of great vision. The powerful insights gained now can be enough to shake the world. Consequently it is important to be fair to all concerned and not unleash power uncontrolled or with selfish aims.

Your creativity in manifesting your vision is great. This should be used to accommodate everyone concerned. The common values of humanity are the issue here. When you take action be sure then of assessing it on the basis of your vision which encompasses all mankind. Contemplation leading to the receptivity of direct insight is the last phase of this change.

Keep open to the needs of others and the collective power will be supportive. Like a reservoir, the deepest human values maintain their supply and purity when the source as well as just distribution is considered. The source of your power now is in persistence in identifying with all of humanity and being disciplined in any self-indulgence.

MAN

For a man, THE ARMY is a change from a deeply arousing condition to a discipline of increasing power so that creative plans can inspire those under you. Once expressed, it is well to be gentle and receptive so that a balanced position can maintain the existing forces. Do not be either too rash nor too lenient. Use force only when absolutely necessary as a last resort.

LINES

—x— 6 When the dispute is over, distribute goods and values appropriately. Don't give unworthy or incapable people positions of power, but reward them materially.

—x— 5 Now is a critical time of benefit to advance an attack if the leader is wise and experienced. Otherwise the costs will be great and to no advantage.

—x— 4 Retreat is honorable when obstacles are insurmountable. A good strategy now is to cease struggle.

—x— 3 Divergent goals or lack of strength is bringing about defeat.

—o— 2 You are the powerful leader of the coming events. Communicate to those subordinate to you in a clear manner and your superiors will benefit you.

—x— 1 Strict discipline is the key to taking action or chaos will follow.

8 UNITY

THE IMAGE

Vast Seas of Sands Condense into Coals of Fire

The belly of the dark EARTH receives waters from the MOUNTAIN held in the hands of the DRAGON.

The woman has conceived and is realising fullness by looking inward. The unborn and the born, the inner and outer are all a UNITY.

EARTHLY MOON CYCLE

Like the in-held breath, the full moon is holding the full power of light in reflection. One is here either on top of things and now can reflect on what has been accomplished, or can sink into delusion. Binary 16.

JUDGMENT

UNITY is the UNION OF THE TIGER AND DRAGON IN THE RECEPTIVE changing into the CONTEMPLATION OF THE DRAGON.

Now is a time wherein forces and people which have been disparate are coming together. This opportunity must be optimally used to align your goals with virtue or what is right from a position of the whole. Use this time to realize more fully the direction of your destiny in relation to your community, culture and global civilization. Widen your perspective to include people of all races, classes and creeds and consider them as part of the unity to which you belong.

WOMAN

For a woman, UNITY is a time of intuitive openness. Trust the flashes of insight that come to you now if they benefit the family, community, nation or mankind as a whole. Bring the best intuitions into action and if in accord with cosmic law, others will join, creating a force and power to manifest a purpose worthy to your understanding.

Feel out your calling, accept it and work with it in actually creating the foundations of a new culture or aspect of it. When great creativity is expressed, many will be summoned to help. Whether you are a leader or helper depends on the durability of your actions in accordance with your intuition.

It does not matter what your position is if the correctness of purpose is agreed upon. Don't hesitate to act, but after you do so, it is beneficial to go into retreat and contemplate the results of your efforts.

MAN

For a man, UNITY is a time of great change of energy. Sexual energy can now be sublimated upward into great inspirational ideas for mankind. If you can consistently transmute grosser energy into more subtle energy and inspiration, you may become a leader among those around you.

Considerations of the needs of others implies not only ideas and active power which can be uniting, but contemplation of the results of actions. If you are working on consistency of transmutation of gross energies, then join with those who have clear directives which benefit mankind as a whole. Persist until consistency endures.

LINES

—x— 6 Unity has passed. You missed the timing. Without giving yourself to others, you will not be served.

—o— 5 Those in accord will surely come together with a powerful aim. A glorious fellowship and fulfillment of projects of priority is imminent. Let the small things go.

—x— 4 Support the leader of your group now and pledge yourself to the common values you share with others.

—x— 3 Cease associating with the people concerned now. Being responsive to the wrong people will be unfortunate.

—x— 2 Don't attempt to influence others by flattery, but only by being true to yourself. Sincerity brings true friendship.

—x— 1 Be faithful in your friendships by being open and honest, then the right people will be attracted to you.

9 FORCE OF SMALL

THE IMAGE

Reflecting Jewels Penetrate into Pure White Light

The eye of the Tiger behind the cloud envisions the FIRE
reaching for the white light of HEAVEN.

The child of consciousness wants to sing and express himself.
The clouds gather like contractions in the throat, but there is
release of desire. As strength rises the breath moves and plants
grow into the sunlight behind the cloud.

HEAVENLY MOON CYCLE

The purification process of the wind above heaven during the waxing half moon brings beneficial times for baths and sweats. Vibrations are so subtle that the moon elixir can penetrate through the membranes of cells. Binary 55.

JUDGMENT

FORCE OF THE SMALL is the INNER TRUTH essence of the TIGER as the feminine principle, centered in the heart of hearts, changing into the CREATIVE. This is a time to be steadfast in the heart during trials. Clouds are forming but there is no release (rain), or direct expression. Keep your thoughts and feeling close to the heart rather than trying to influence others at this time. It is a time to keep strong impulses in check until the times change.

This is a good time to prepare for a large undertaking. You will eventually have great responsibility and perhaps will be the guide of a group of people. Attend to your inner attitudes, intentions and the resources to execute your plans will come at the right time. You might undertake small tasks now in preparation for larger ones.

MAN

For a man, FORCE OF THE SMALL creates a great compression of energy or yang potential, but it is not expressed or released. Now is not a time to say or do much, but to hold close to the present situation as a potential for the future.

WOMAN

For a woman, FORCE OF THE SMALL is a positive potential energy, but not a time to release this energy. For the woman at this time, the sex center is like a reservoir to do and fulfill and manifest, but it is not now time to take action. It is best to keep from imagining scenarios of action. Just be with the present potential. It is very positive as long as the dam at the reservoir is not broken. Keep your reserve.

LINES

—o— 6 Rain refreshes everyone now. Rest at this time. The effort is fulfilled. Pushing forward brings danger.

—o— 5 Sincerity with others brings mutual regeneration of resources. All will thereby be fulfilled that needs to be.

—x— 4 Being honest and open dissolves fear. Only the truth deeply influences others.

—o— 3 Pushing on by force will destroy the house. Passion unabated creates chaos.

—o— 2 Retreat into your true nature and, by natural affinity, all that is needed will come.

—o— 1 If you are straying from your path, come back to the Tao, your true nature.

10 TREADING

THE IMAGE

Streaming Jewels Explode into White Light

The head of the white light of HEAVEN reflects in the FLAMING eyes of the Tiger.

The innocent child of consciousness treads on the tail of the Tiger. The child is in danger between two sources of power, but since he does not know it, there is innocence. The beginning of song springs from desire.

HEAVENLY MOON CYCLE

Power is held in check by the conflict of abundant spiritual radiance and abusive self-power. Accept grace from heaven but take nothing from those below. Increasing moon elixir. Binary 59.

JUDGMENT

The Tiger's tail is trodden on because the full CREATIVE diminishes to the dark line in the center where the essence of the INNER TRUTH OF THE TIGER is realized in the heart.

This is an inspiring time, but one of danger, for the time after the copulation of the Tiger and the Dragon is one wherein one's destiny can change in an instant. One must consider the best interests of those around and not only what one desires. It could be a highly reactive time, for the creative energies are withdrawing and one is to come to a realization of Inner Truth.

MAN

For a man, TREADING is a change from inspirational ideas to a deflation of energies to a more contemplative attitude and deep inner turning to what the heart says.

The deep heart knows and it is only a matter of feeling and listening to it. Like a full exhale, it is time to inhale new awareness of Self. It is particularly dangerous to try to mock creativity or greatness when the expressive energy has subsided. Go inward and purify in the fires of the heart.

WOMAN

For a woman, TREADING is a time when sexually aroused, but this is not a time for dissipation of energy. That could be dangerous indeed. It is time to allow the sexual energies to turn inward and enrich the whole inner life like a pure fountain which now is spread throughout the land and irrigates otherwise parched pastures!

The fountain of energies can then be made regenerative rather than simply a release. The 'Tiger of the Heart' finds itself in love with everyone now, but outward behaviour needs to be in accordance with tradition and social acceptance. In other words, the conduits of resurgent energy which nourish others need to be laid in accepted patterns. Then a woman can influence in subtle ways, without any devious appearance at all.

LINES

—O— 6 Examine your own conduct. If others have benefitted by it, you can already see your good fortune.

—O— 5 Perilous dangers abound, but by firm resolution, you will succeed in an accomplishment.

—O— 4 Now is a time to proceed carefully. There is danger, but you have inner strength now which will carry you through.

—X— 3 When one is half-blind and weak is no time to be a warrior. You may feel overly confident and not see the present danger.

—O— 2 Moderation and balance create an even course. Seek neither ambition nor laziness.

—O— 1 Follow your accustomed path. Basic values will lead you to your goal. Solitude and simplicity are beneficial.

11 PEACE

THE IMAGE

Reflecting Caves and Valleys Penetrate into White Light

The feet of the Dragon running on THUNDER becomes the LAKE reflected in the mouth of the Tiger.

Like the center of a cyclone, PEACE has intense calm in the middle of powerful activity. Heaven and earth unite at every horizon creating critical lines of fusion.

EARTHLY MOON CYCLE

Almost at waxing half moon, PEACE is the balance of earth mirroring in heaven. The moon elixir brings intense serenity. Binary 7.

JUDGMENT

PEACE is the change from the APPROACH OF THE DRAGON to the POWER OF THE GREAT OF THE TIGER. This is a small but harmonious transformation. The masculine and feminine principles are in balance, but they are not fused at this time. Each considers the other as a balance to the whole. This is like springtime when the yang, strong light forces are rising from below.

This is one of the transitional 'time' golden hexagrams in the cycle of the year which corresponds to the first month, east and 3–5 a.m. So it is a time of poised new beginnings and energy is ascending.

The harmonizing energy present now is a great foundation for the growth and prosperity of all things. Take responsibility and use the available resources for the common good. Spiritual energies are readily available from the springs of selfless love. Cultivate your best personal growth by helping others and help others by self-cultivation. Self-worth is synonymous with valuing others just as they are. Now is a beneficial time to practise this truth.

MAN

For a man, PEACE represents a change of the subtle current at the base of the spine up to the middle of the back to the throat. There is an intensity in this small change, for it is transformation wherein the APPROACH OF THE DRAGON which represents the thunderous arousing energy is rising into the POWER OF THE GREAT OF THE TIGER. These are both powerful and active tendencies. There is an opportunity here to balance the lower 'instinctual' forces and the higher 'insightful' forces.

WOMAN

For a woman, PEACE represents a change of the subtle current from the third eye of inner vision to the solar plexus center where the fiery energies of the subtle circulation are stored. This implies that her PEACE is towards creative manifestation and the advancement of culture. That which needs reform is to be eradicated in the progressive movement of refreshing insights and activities. Prosperity follows Peace.

LINES

—x— 6 Vigilance is needed when guards are down. Maintain restraint and hold your position of benefit or there will be chaos.

—x— 5 Joy and success are here found by receiving the help of those below you. If you can be central and balanced, the aim is accomplished for everyone's benefit.

—x— 4 Friends will come if you share what you have. Cease seeking fruits from your efforts, but enjoy the intrinsic value of working for a worthy goal.

—o— 3 Enjoy the presence of the present and persevere in what is right. Endure difficulties with equanimity.

—o— 2 Patience with others, resolution, distant vision and self-reliance enable you to walk gently in the middle.

—o— 1 One action follows another. By a good beginning, others will be attracted by what you do, and also contribute.

☰12 STANDSTILL

THE IMAGE

Streaming Jewels Explode into Coals of Fire

The quiet WIND allows the sleeping Tiger to rest on thighs while the hands of the Dragon reach for the MOUNTAIN.

Heaven stands far above and the earth sinks down and the trees bend under the weight of the past. Disengaging separations brings a pause towards inward consciousness. Swamps are places of incubation.

HEAVENLY MOON CYCLE

What is outward is inverse to what is inward. Though heaven and earth stand apart, there is integration through the moon elixir. The body is illumined from within the day after the waxing half moon. Binary 56.

JUDGMENT

STANDSTILL is the change of the RETREAT OF THE TIGER into the CONTEMPLATION OF THE DRAGON.

This is a time to go very deeply within and not attempt to make connections in the world. There are people with inferior motives in power and they cannot be beneficially fought directly at this time.

There is an impasse now and it is best to retreat and contemplate the significance of true values. Words and actions are useless now for those in power have no inclination for the truth. Don't waste energy in trying to change either your environment or other people, but go within and affirm all that you know to be just and right.

WOMAN

For a woman, STANDSTILL is a time of rising intuition through a disengagement from all outside affairs. Do not accept enticing offers from people in power now, for their offers have strings attached. There are misunderstandings on all levels and the best thing to do is to apply further discipline to your own inner development.

Your intuition of what is right is on the ascent now, so use this time to further it through meditation and practices which bring you into accord with the sources of life. The effects of life are impossible to deal with and chaotic, so remove yourself from them until the time passes.

MAN

For a man, STANDSTILL is a time of deep penetrating inner vision if he can go deeply within himself. This vision will bring forth the needed reserves of energy through a contemplative repose. The energy fields will build and develop out of an all-encompassing acceptance of this disengaging situation. Be content to have no outward power at all at this time, for 'Heaven' and 'Earth' are out of accord.

LINES

6 Adversity and standstill can be removed by resolute purpose. A great reversal leading to felicity is at hand!

5 Vigilance! A deep firm root of truth in the heart will change stagnation now.

4 Adverse circumstances are now powerful means to achieve high goals. People of virtue will support your effort to act in accord with the cosmic order.

3 If your motives are not pure, there will be shame and humiliation.

2 When there is injustice, there is temporary benefit to inferior people, but it will not last. Accept temporary stagnation and stand aloof from it.

1 When changes are adverse, remain calm and centered. Many are disturbed by the change and everything falls however it may by its own nature.

13 FELLOWSHIP

THE IMAGE

Rainbow Jewels Vaporize into Lightning

The thighs of the Tiger pounce through the WIND before the pure white light of HEAVEN.

The womb is dark within a radiating body. The dark core of the clear fire reveals the inner unity of all things amidst distinct species and kinds. Resonance is the deep empathy of sentience.

HEAVENLY MOON CYCLE

The great blessing of the radiance of the moon elixir brings one in FELLOWSHIP with all of life. The separation of clan, caste, religion, color, creed amplifies the universal equality when the moon is nearly full. Binary 61.

JUDGMENT

FELLOWSHIP is the RETREAT OF THE TIGER changing into the CREATIVE COPULATION OF THE TIGER AND DRAGON. This indicates a time to allow collective energy to flow and realize the harmonies in relationships of all kinds. The feminine principle is at first retreating and then advancing. The masculine principle is at first strong and then accommodating.

MAN

For a man, there is a focus on vision and imagination at this time, to find the cosmic order and to see the place of everyone involved in the present situation. A community may be forming, based on fraternity and common ideals. It is therefore important for a man to have a clear vision which is unwavering. To do this, he must allow the feminine principle within himself to work intuitively and to trust his vision as long as it is not based on selfish desire, but the common good.

This vision, for a man, is a complete revolution of subtle energy flow and is the process needed to harmonize all the centers. See the different elements and persons in the present situation in a large overview. From this overview of harmony and order, a community can form and take creative action. It is a time to begin new endeavours, but only if the good of the whole is seen.

WOMAN

For a woman, it is a time to allow your energies to rise from the spleen center up the back so that you can become totally receptive and intuitive. Then you will have a vision of the whole and can begin to exercise disciplines in the social structure which will be in accord with the cosmic order. If you are receptive enough it will be a time of magnificent creativity for the social order and cultural fulfillment. A woman can fulfill through action, in harmony with a man's vision and ideas at this time.

LINES

—o— 6 A rural setting for a meeting now is insignificant, but certainly not a mistake. The aim is good, but don't expect much.

—o— 5 In powerful meetings, strong emotions are expressed, but remaining true to virtue will dissolve any conflict. Both parties will then laugh.

—o— 4 Your wild vision is out of accord with community interests. Your own confusion will suffer you to correct your actions. Then benefits will abound.

—o— 3 Cease ambition with those of hidden motives. Your opponent is strong and it is well to cease any cunning and crafty ways.

—x— 2 Don't be an elitist. Exclusive ways will not bring about a great idea. Go beyond an ingrown 'family'.

—o— 1 Leave your privacy and go out to meet people now. Come together openly with people and those of like mind will find benefit in your sharing the treasures of wisdom you have found in solitude.

14 POSSESSION IN GREAT MEASURE

THE IMAGE

Rainbow Mountains Vaporize into White Light

The pure white light radiates throughout HEAVEN into the mouth of the Tiger where all is reflected in the LAKE.

Consciousness moves into the womb of light where the invisible is made visible. Seeing broadly is seeing in empathy with everything 'just as it is'. Clairvoyance decreases with distinctions of good and evil.

HEAVENLY MOON CYCLE

GREAT POSSESSIONS is the dark moon and the culmination of the moon elixir in the higher body. Like a seed or kernel, it holds the pattern of all that is to be, but in itself is invisible. The dark heavenly moon is one's greatest inner wealth. Binary 47.

JUDGMENT

In GREAT POSSESSIONS we see the positive CREATIVE principle, wherein the Tiger and Dragon are fused, turn into the POWER OF THE GREAT OF THE TIGER.

Here is the feminine principle coming to the fore as an unbiased force. It is a time to realize the non-reality of the ego and the supremacy of 'Heaven' and its intelligence. That this is born through the feminine principle does not make it personal or biased, but rather a cosmic power. Creative inspiration is flowing now. Move with it.

MAN

For a man, this change is great indeed, for it involves an awakening of the 'Jade Gate' in the back of the head to great creativity. The subtle current rises from there over the crown and descends with a contemplative feeling. As the subtle current enters the central channel where heart and brain reside, it descends again to become arousing energy for outer activity. Now it rises up the back to the root of the heart and throat chakras. Here a man knows what to do. You can now be unselfish, kind and gentle and yet powerful. Coming from the heart of the great feminine awakening within yourself, others can now trust and give you power because of your innate goodness.

WOMAN

Equally, for a woman, the change of the subtle current is dramatic as an inner transformation. It begins with the creative awakening of her sexual center which immediately ascends into the deep central channel through the heart and brain. In the descent of the subtle current, you may feel quiet, and as it ascends from the base of the spine up the back, you may become more and more receptive. This open attitude clears your body and mind of any self-opinionated desires. You can examine yourself for signs of aggression or pride or dominance. This inner cleansing is essential to create the conditions of great purity for receiving the intuition and visions which in the descending current are linked with the fire of the blood. This purification now becomes a rich reservoir of energy in the solar plexus center where the POWER OF THE GREAT OF THE TIGER reveals itself. This is a time for a woman to conserve her energies and shine forth in her inmost integrity and true compassion.

LINES

—O— 6 Keep balance and a good sense of proportion especially amidst great blessings and good fortune. Because wisdom expects nothing it receives great benefits.

—X— 5 Your integrity of character brings spontaneous words and actions born of truth. This brings power and influence to you. Others will follow soon.

—O— 4 Discriminate what is too much and what is too little and don't attempt to compete with others. Expansion will bring remorse.

—O— 3 Give up petty concerns and place your resources at the disposal of an enlightened leader or worthy cause.

—O— 2 Now is a time to advance powerfully. Your reserves of energy and money enable you to truly move with your aims now.

—O— 1 Making no great advances leaves no possibility of mistakes. No trouble and no benefit are yours now.

15 MODESTY

THE IMAGE

Reflecting Caves and Valleys Penetrate into Coals of Fire

The belly of the dark EARTH receives the RAIN of nourishment silently falling into the ears of the Dragon.

The earth lies low and sends influences up to heaven through the mountain. Heaven rains down nectar to earth. Silence in music and speech makes meaning. Stillness and humility within the winter cave opens the heart.

EARTHLY MOON CYCLE

The mid-point of the waxing half moon brings the augmentation and diminution of activities in balanced accord. Open consciousness in an inconspicuous profile. Binary 4.

JUDGMENT

In MODESTY the union of the Tiger and Dragon in the RECEPTIVE changes into the HUMBLE VIGILANCE OF THE DRAGON.

This is a good time to maintain a low profile and be inconspicuous in your aims and actions. Receptivity is your main attitude. This can be a deep fusion process with the universe. By being receptive and open you will see a vast scheme of events and thereby know what adjustments are necessary.

MODESTY is a time to attune to nature in both her fine spiritual essences and her outward forms. To know the relationship of the subtle and gross, of the large and the small, of the inner and outer is part of the perspective received now. If something is too large for its place, it is well to diminish its effect and vice versa. To know the difference between a source and effect is essential. Thereby you can see what is to be carried through to the end and what is to be released.

WOMAN

For a woman, MODESTY is a great transformation from open, intuitive receptivity to powerfully arousing creative endeavours. Everything that is worldly can be accomplished but without willful effort. The main thing is to enjoy the dark open void of unknowing which brings intuitive vision and avoid trying to bring about certainty where there is none.

You will have all the resources and helpers needed if you can be selfless. Once the vision is clear, don't hold back your newly given power to manifest. As it comes forth, it will eventually also be released. So then do whatever is necessary to balance the situation. If someone needs scolding do so. If someone needs encouragement, support them. A humbly attentive attitude without personal biases will bring about justice to every situation you enter into now.

As a woman, MODESTY is not a time to remain in the closet, but to be both intuitive and active. Being in the open and hidden are both compatible with this creative process.

MAN

For a man, MODESTY may be difficult if he is used to being in the limelight and being outspoken. For it is best to remain receptive and these processes are sometimes even unconscious to a man. It is indeed a process of bringing the unconscious strata of your being into consciousness. What was formerly full needs to be emptied and then the empty will be filled from sources beyond self-will.

A sense of balance and moderation are essential now. Through your sense of fairness, you will find supporters for the work to be done without having to wave banners. Do not attempt to lay down laws or titles, but allow everything to take its course with true humility.

LINES

—x— 6 Confusion around you need not bother you. Use self-discipline and express humility with great energy and the offenders will realize their shame.

—x— 5 Firm decision about worthy goals for all concerned needs to be powerfully acted upon. Now is a time of severity in modesty.

—x— 4 Move on with your work in all humility and continue in a worthy direction.

—o— 3 Accept hard work in a modest attitude and complete the task at hand. The dedicated succeed.

—x— 2 Inner composure expresses itself without postures or expectations. Continue with humble efforts.

—x— 1 Quiet selfless endeavors go far. Claim nothing, but remain steadfast and simple in your endeavors.

16 ENTHUSIASM

THE IMAGE

Streaming Mountains Explode into Coals of Fire

The ears of the Dragon receive reverberations of music above the WATERS lapping around the belly of the dark EARTH.

The whole body gives support to the song resounding out of the earth. Thunder and rain bring a rhythm to the circulation of consciousness. Awaken! The Muses of Inspiration are here!

EARTHLY MOON CYCLE

The light of the moon has reached a mid-point. The inbreath of winter has burst into the buzzing vibrations of spring. Dance on the waters of life. Binary 8.

JUDGMENT

ENTHUSIASM is the transformation of the HUMBLE VIGILANCE OF THE DRAGON into the RECEPTIVE UNION OF THE TIGER AND DRAGON.

This is a time of devotion whereby many together are humbled by the magnitude of movements occurring in society now. There is a harmony found within the quiet center of all and it is this harmony which inspires devotion now.

Go deeply within and place yourself in humble service to mankind. This inner harmony will bring people into accord with cosmic law and bring about changes which instill a true transmission of spiritual heritage. Sacred music and dance are appropriate now for it is by inner harmonization and resonance that everything will be initiated on its proper course.

This is a time of expressions which are in harmony with a universal spirit of peace. There are laws of octaves and correspondences upon which the universe functions. This is an invisible network of proportions and resonances whereby everything in the universe sings in harmony with everything else, within its deepest being.

WOMAN

For a woman, ENTHUSIASM is a time of bringing what is sometimes known as the Kundalini up into the head whereby awakening can occur. This is the natural course of the Tao at the right time. Don't attempt to express your feelings outwardly now, but bring all subtle currents up into a distillation and integration process.

Your devotion to common ideals of humanity springs from a real source. Allow this devotion to open up all blocks which separate you from others. Inspiration will well up from the depths of your heart which will bring about an inward harmonization of people involved in your present life.

All you need to do is keep in harmony with your true nature.

The Tao will do all the rest. If you are inwardly inspired to conduct or help in a ritual which unites inwardly, feel free to do so.

MAN

For a man, ENTHUSIASM is a time of great transformation. It is nothing less than bringing the deepest vibrations of one's physical body, emotions, mind and intuition into harmonization. This is a rising current from the fundamental waters of vital life into a rush of power and creative expression, prompted by the deepest inspirations of cosmic order. Music, dance, theater and all arts celebrating the pure resonance inherent in the invisible language of Tao are relevant expressions. Bring this expression into a contemplative receptivity and allow the harmony brought about to resonate continuously in the silence.

LINES

6 Excessive enthusiasm and enjoyment must be moderated. If you have delusions, a sober awakening is awaiting you.

5 Too much enthusiasm can be a disease. Awareness of your own reserves of energy will prevent further dissipation. Return to responsibilities.

4 Express your vision and others will be attracted to form a well-founded fellowship. Your sincerity can be relied on and will bring helpers for a great undertaking.

3 Try to please no one. Others' views on you are not a beneficial source of your action. Don't hesitate to approach one in authority now, but in so doing, remain true to yourself.

2 Remain unswerving in your integrity and direction despite the dazzle of fame or benefits. Neither flattery nor neglect are of any merit.

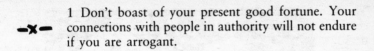

1 Don't boast of your present good fortune. Your connections with people in authority will not endure if you are arrogant.

17 FOLLOWING

THE IMAGE

Streaming Sands Explode into Lightning

The ears of the Dragon hear the WATERS becoming
FLAMES in the eyes of the Tiger.

Moving with change is passing through the eyes and ears of
opposites and receiving the power of emptiness. Accept what is
happening and follow the currents.

EARTHLY MOON CYCLE

Once resonance is established, the right movements imply accord. Just after the waning half moon, knowing what to do is just being. Binary 25.

JUDGMENT

FOLLOWING is one of the eight totally transformative golden hexagrams. Here the HUMBLE VIGILANCE OF THE DRAGON changes into the INNER TRUTH OF THE TIGER. Adaptation of the feminine and masculine principles to each other is primary now.

MAN AND WOMAN

The change of the subtle current is within the central channel for both men and women. This represents a complete internal change from the watery abdominal and emotional centers into the heart and into the brain.

This indicates a time to release old prejudices, resentments, opinions or errors of judgment and to allow the freshness of intuition to guide one.

The circumstances may be difficult but this is not a time to resist or fight, nor is it a time to retreat. Rather, it is well to leave the control to others and adapt to the situation. If you are in a position of a leader, then to find a following it is necessary to adjust one's desires to the welfare of the whole.

Being flexible is doing all one can within the social milieu. A low profile in leadership is appropriate. This is not being secretive but harmonizing with existing conditions. Service to others is not servile, but in harmony with the common good.

The heart is the harmonizer and its quality is INNER TRUTH. By allowing the head to be an administrator through humble awareness, the heart as direct intuition and harmonization can function and know the correct place for all. There is peace through harmony.

LINES

—x— 6 Your wisdom is needed to guide a worthy leader. Since he is faithful to your wisdom, your selfless service at this time is very beneficial.

—o— 5 Keep high visions and persist in accomplishing them with faithful effort. This will bring great benefits.

—o— 4 Don't be deceived about those who follow you for ulterior motives. Keep clear your aims and act with virtue even if it means independence.

—x— 3 Release the small and unworthy so that you can find what is of great value to you and others. Be firm with your decision to ally with the great.

—x— 2 If you are stubborn about clinging to small projects and people of little value, how will you be free to connect with the great?

—o— 1 Dramatic changes can bring out your virtues. Go out and make friends with people of integrity.

18 WORK ON DECAY

THE IMAGE

Reflecting Mountains Penetrate into Comets and Stars

The eyes of the Tiger glow in the autumnal mute FIRES transmuting into WATERY vibrations through the ears of the Dragon.

Every fruit is a new seed when the useless decays and the useful is allowed to work. Blind spots are eyes which have not yet seen. The past is energy for the future.

HEAVENLY MOON CYCLE

During DECAY it is necessary to work consciously on what needs healing and reform. Even in the meditation of receiving the moon elixir one cannot leave everything to the effortless! Binary 38.

JUDGMENT

WORK ON WHAT HAS BEEN SPOILED reveals a total transformation which is that of the INNER TRUTH OF THE TIGER into the HUMBLE VIGILANCE OF THE DRAGON.

This is a time which needs drastic attention and a willingness to change yourself and the situation totally. Now is a time to work, but only if insight is there and a willingness to admit where in the past you have made errors. The quicker you acknowledge the state of disrepair, the easier it will be to remedy it.

There has been an excess of some kind in the past and it has spoiled the inner growth. Effort and insight are needed to remedy the situation. This is a hexagram of great regenerative power. Use it to turn the energy from disintegration towards an integrated whole.

WOMAN AND MAN

For both men and women, WORK ON WHAT HAS BEEN SPOILED is a time wherein the reserves of energy have not been used properly and corruption has set in. Purification of body, feelings and mind is necessary so that either stagnant surplus energy or lack of energy can be balanced. Eat only pure foods and only in small or moderate amounts. If you are sluggish or toxic, fasting at this time would be in order.

Place your thoughts with your highest aims. Think of the boundless gifts of the sun and find the luminous source within your heart. Allow the power of your own inner truth to come to bear on the situation. This is a time of catharsis. Forgive and be forgiven.

When you surrender to the inner truth, insight spontaneously will come and you will know what to do. The task may seem overwhelming, but if you now look within your heart, you will realize that, step by step, obstacles will be overcome and wounds, divisions, decay and spoilation of all kinds will be removed.

This is, above all, not a time of complacency or rationalization. Energetic processes are needed to allow the insights on the situation to be activated. Deliberation is needed only for clarity and then disciplined action needs to be taken. More and more energy and inspiration will come as you take action in accord with the inner truth of the matter.

LINES

—O— 6 It is wise now to withdraw from the mundane aspect of the situation and serve only noble purposes.

—X— 5 You are chosen to bring about a successful reform and if you proceed, you will be supported, praised and honored.

—X— 4 Cease being indecisive about taking action to reform the corruption from past mistakes in relationships. This is useless and humiliating.

—O— 3 Don't be too vigorous in changing corruption from the past on the paternal side of your family.

—O— 2 Neither excess nor rigidity will correct the spoilation from the maternal side of your family. Continue with moderate reform of your life.

—X— 1 Something corrupt in your past relationship with father or uncles can be remedied now, but with difficulty. Cautious reform.

☷☳ 19 APPROACH

THE IMAGE

Vast Seas of Caves and Valleys Condense into White Light

The feet of the Dragon electrify the THUNDEROUS clouds issuing lightning.

The contractions of the mother giving birth are felt for miles around. The advancing waves become great and break upon the distant shore.

EARTHLY MOON CYCLE

The light of the moon is increasing and you can continue with plans, prospects and activities. Binary 3.

JUDGMENT

APPROACH is the immutable golden hexagram of the APPROACH OF THE DRAGON. This indicates a time of positive movement and creative insight. Opportunities are opening up in business, relationships and resources. Energy is increasing like spring thunder showers.

Don't hesitate to allow energetic changes in various parts of your life now. Vigorous measures may be taken, but only if you consider all persons and elements concerned. Balance is needed when approaching people in authority or with whom you wish to make changes. Motivation is a primary issue when dynamic advances are made. Otherwise energy expenditures will have gone to waste. Internal and external growth are mutually beneficial when in harmony. Control and guidance are needed when you seek advances.

MAN

For a man, APPROACH is a time to allow spiritual and physical strength to mount. This is best used in self-realization and social nourishment, but not in passionate expression. One's whole society and environment can benefit from this time if you can give your attention and energy to it.

WOMAN

For a woman, APPROACH is a time to see the potentiality of future blossoms in whatever she is involved with. She is wise to use this time for getting clear the future mode of action and communicate it to others.

LINES

—x— 6 Your sincerity and generosity will benefit everyone. Such mature advancement brings a moment of greatness.

—x— 5 Excellent practices of balance and harmony for the common good now leads to sovereign work. You are trusted.

—x— 4 Your advances are appropriate now. Continue in your present approach and use this easy time to benefit all concerned.

—x— 3 Now that all is running smoothly, don't abuse your power, for your promotion must endure trials. There is danger in over-confidence.

—o— 2 Go ahead with your proposal, for your ideals are in accord with cosmic law. This is a time of great support and benefit.

—o— 1 It is very beneficial to approach without partiality. Continue serving according to your principles.

20 CONTEMPLATION

THE IMAGE

Vast Seas of Jewels Condense into Coals of Fire

The hands of the Dragon grasp the vital source of themselves through the stillness of the MOUNTAIN.

With vision and compassion the strength is found within the core of the tree where what was once sun becomes an offering of flame. Spirit is born of the mastery of life.

HEAVENLY MOON CYCLE

The day after dark moon brings the moon elixir into a refined distillation. Contemplate the course of your life and you will be seen for what you are. Binary 48.

JUDGMENT

CONTEMPLATION is one of the immutable golden hexagrams. The CONTEMPLATION OF THE DRAGON is an unchanging state whereby sincere attention brings deeper and deeper consciousness through purification.

Use this time to reflect on your life and the lives of those around you as examples of cosmic law. Disengage from personal attachments and allow people and circumstances to become objects of meditation. Look within and find the sources of the present situation in previous thoughts and actions.

If you can master your own desires, attachments and revulsions, you are well on the way to becoming one with cosmic law. Everything in nature and civilization is a sign like a page in the book of life. By realizing what is immutable and what is changing, what is moving into unified states and what is moving into disintegration, you will be able to have mastery over your life and inspire others also.

WOMAN

For a woman, it is now more important to make an effort to discipline the body, emotions and mind so that through practices, intuitions will arise spontaneously. The currents are rising and it is well to realize the tendency of movements now. Take this opportunity to evaluate the past which will enable you to know the trend of the future.

You may become prominent among those around you now and it is important not to identify this prominence with your personal self. Rather it is the insights from your contemplations which are the center of focus. This can bring about great cooperation to a common goal which then can become widespread.

MAN

For a man, CONTEMPLATION is a time to allow fugitive thoughts and intuitions about life to create an energy field valuable for future use. These intuitions are more right than you may have previously believed. Express them to the best of your ability and you will be trusted because of the truth of what you say. This is a good time to meditate, but also to express insights which come through your meditations. Most of this will be accomplished without great effort now.

LINES

—O— 6 Now you have enough experience that you can realistically contemplate your life and truly evaluate who you are.

—O— 5 Since you are in a position of authority, it is important that your actions accord with your words and values so that you provide an example for others.

—x— 4 By contemplating many different perspectives you can now transcend your personal viewpoint and influence others to the benefit of all concerned.

—x— 3 You need to become decisive about broadening and deepening your viewpoint so that your life will move meaningfully forward. Discipline is needed.

—x— 2 A timid perspective will not win respect. Have the courage to view things from the vantage of a greater whole than your personal positions.

—x— 1 A childish viewpoint is not appropriate to you now. Superficial contemplation will not lead anywhere.

21 BITING THROUGH

THE IMAGE

Streaming Mountains Explode into Lightning

The thighs of the Tiger move on the WIND becoming the THUNDEROUS feet of the Dragon.

The equanimous heart cuts through karmic knots by cosmic law. When the heart is still, energy is found for what needs to be done.

HEAVENLY MOON CYCLE

Courageous faith is brought by the waning half moon elixir. The power to see beyond the conscious mind is the power to fulfill whatever arises, however irksome. Binary 41.

JUDGMENT

BITING THROUGH is one of the totally changing golden hexagrams and is a change from the RETREAT OF THE TIGER to the APPROACH OF THE DRAGON. These are diametric opposites of both feminine and masculine principles and their retreating and advancing motions.

Now is a time for radical change and energetic reform. This is nothing less than the beginning of the negentropic process of life and order against the decaying process of time. There are obstacles and the tendencies of the dissolution of energy, but one must now realize the cosmic law of reciprocity and adhere to it strictly. This will enable one to cut through the obstacles and support superior character and punish inferior character.

MAN

For a man, BITING THROUGH is a time wherein the vision of clarity of what and how to make reforms is brought into contemplation. From such contemplation, the situation is irradiated with inner light and brought down into active work. If one has seen clearly what the situation is, it cannot be either ignored or justified. Action according to fairness to all parties concerned can now successfully be taken.

WOMAN

For a woman, BITING THROUGH may be a radical cutting through of delusions and clingings and an awakening to the reality of the situation. An out-and-out surrender to the highest wisdom is essential to receive the intuition and vision which arouses people nearby to the needed reform.

A woman here can be a model of selflessness and uncompromising truth. She may function as an oracle, either by speaking or being silent, but above all, living her vision of truth.

LINES

—O— 6 If you are blind to your own stubbornness, how can you expect to be delivered from suffering? It is unfortunate you won't listen.

—X— 5 Keep centered as you proceed through the storm of the difficult task and your firmness will vanquish the ordeal.

—O— 4 The time is difficult, but you are up to the task and must gain courage to be strong and persevering, for difficulties cannot be avoided. Trying to avoid them will make things worse.

—X— 3 The present position is poisonous for a good reason. Stop criticizing others who have deep-rooted problems and the poison will no longer come back to you.

—X— 2 Effective punishment is needed to reform bad habits and form good ones. Swift retribution is a blessing. Admit your mistakes and correct them.

—O— 1 Restrain your own stubbornness and aggressiveness. Self-discipline is necessary or you will suffer punishment and immobility.

22 GRACE

THE IMAGE

Reflecting Mountains Penetrate into Lightning

The Hands of the Dragon contemplate the MOUNTAIN reflected in the LAKE. The Tiger's mouth mirrors what is above.

Karmic law has a beauty of form: justice above mirroring actions below. Reaping is according to sowing.

HEAVENLY MOON CYCLE

The moon elixir has begun to flow within. Now is the continued point of non-doing out of the great stillness of the mountain. Binary 37.

JUDGMENT

GRACE is one of the completely changing golden hexagrams wherein the CONTEMPLATION OF THE DRAGON becomes the POWER OF THE GREAT OF THE TIGER. This is a perfect, balanced poise, like the Tiger crouching in beautiful form. Here is the supreme essence of the Tiger as beauty.

In daily life, GRACE is a time of all-pervasive neutral serenity of heart and mind. There is now no ambition and no regret. This is a moment of the perfection of form. Outer circumstances can be appreciated for exactly what they are. Although awareness of a public image is far from your mind just now, it is nevertheless of importance to now appear graceful in public. Social intercourse and love are in ideal form and all aspects of the arts can be accomplished now. This is a time of effortless effort, not radical or extreme ideas or intense emotions.

MAN

For a man, GRACE is the transition of the subtle current from the solar plexus center wherein there is a contemplative quality, down to the sexual center. This is the negative pole of a man and now is a time to allow sensuous awareness to be experienced. A sense of luxury is good now but also it can be a danger if in excess. As the subtle current moves up into the central channel of brain and heart, there is a purification. As it descends to the base of the spine and up to the middle of the upper back and throat there is a glow which may awaken a sense of romantic love. Finding expression for this love creates beauty.

WOMAN

For a woman, GRACE is a change of the subtle current from the cool nerve plexus in the back of the throat up over the crown and down to the solar plexus. This is an awakening of a feeling of being 'in tune' with the times. Now is a good time to be at the right place at the right time. You can be clear about relationships of values now and can give fair statements. The parts of the whole can be seen to work harmoniously together. A harmonizer of whatever is immediate, you can be trusted to be fair and find goodness and beauty all around you. This is not a time to make long-range plans, however.

LINES

—O— 6 Give up seeking high offices and signs of recognition. If you remain true to yourself, then all that is needed will be yours.

—X— 5 Someone with whom you would like a lasting relationship is not impressed with grand offerings. Sincere feelings are the greatest gift in this case.

—X— 4 Honesty and sincerity are the best adornments now. Do not seek external show, but stay with simplicity and self-knowledge.

—O— 3 Grace and charm are yours now, but do not replace natural virtues and principles with surface culture and the pleasures of decorative fantasies.

—X— 2 Substance in your life is what you need, not symbols of worth. Forget outward appearances and cultivate courage and righteousness.

—O— 1 Move by your own feet and do not seek decorated vehicles. Rely on yourself for now.

23 SPLITTING APART

THE IMAGE

Vast Seas of Mountains Condense into Coals of Fire

The hands of the Dragon grasp MOUNTAINS of roots and seeds in the belly of the dark EARTH.

Sinking deeply into acceptance the pregnant seed splits by the force of new life. Die to be reborn.

HEAVENLY MOON CYCLE

The inner path opens the day after full moon whereby the moon elixir seeds itself in the darkness. Binary 32.

JUDGMENT

SPLITTING APART is the CONTEMPLATION OF THE DRAGON changing into the RECEPTIVE UNION OF THE TIGER AND DRAGON.

Now is a time to realize that only by dying to all clinging is complete realization possible. You may feel undermined or in a deteriorating condition, but this is natural at this time. Accept and go within to find the immutability which comes with receptivity.

It is time to give up all attachments and aims and you will find a truth and tranquility which comes only when all dependence on outward circumstances is allowed to fall away.

Don't attempt to improve your situation at this time. Just allow to happen whatever will. Continue to be benevolent even to those who, out of ignorance, hasten to take from you whatever they can. Nurture yourself inwardly with contemplation of everything you are witnessing, without making judgments. This is a time to submit, be silent and remain open to the wisdom that comes to you.

WOMAN

For a woman, SPLITTING APART is a time when high intuition is almost reached. All that needs to be done is to persist in attention to life. Be a witness to the dissolving of holdings you thought were secure and make no attempt to run after them.

Your contemplation of all that has happened to you will give way to complete open receptivity. At that moment a subtle understanding and wisdom will by far outdo any apparent sacrifices you have had to make.

Cease identifying with what you previously valued and realize that the truth is broad and great enough to cover all of humanity. Your devotion which is born of inner stillness will bring you the immutable spirit which cannot be touched by any circumstance whatsoever.

MAN

For a man, SPLITTING APART is a loss of outward reserves of energy and, if dealt with in a spirit of acceptance, renewal will be born of it. If you have the benevolence and devotion to bear this time in equanimity, your inner strength will be greater for future undertakings. Only when the seed dies to itself does it sprout forth the shoot which can grow into a mighty tree.

Through your increasing emptiness at this time you can realize the immutable serenity which cannot be harmed. Destruction and creation are two poles of one process of inner and outer development. Bring yourself to a total receptivity and acceptance of all that comes and you will find all that is unnecessary falls away of its own accord.

LINES   •

—o— 6 Power can return now to people of vision. If you are not self-indulgent and are a leader, you can help now. Evil eventually consumes itself.

—x— 5 Possibilities are opening now to change a corrupt situation. Cooperate with others of sincerity for the mutual benefit of all opposing factions.

—x— 4 Corruption is very close and is entering your own body. Danger is past the point of return. Accept and wait.

—x— 3 Remaining true to yourself even while amidst external corruption and difficulty will strengthen your character. Stick to truth whether others do or not.

—x— 2 Wishful thinking does not produce clarity or strength. Caution. Do not remain near cruel influences. Adapt as best you can until you can free yourself.

—x— 1 Sleepless nights or bad dreams indicate the beginning of danger. For now just be alert and wait, for inferior elements have already entered the situation.

24 RETURN

THE IMAGE

Vast Seas of Caves and Valleys Condense into Lightning

The belly of the dark EARTH receives the return of the THUNDEROUS feet of the Dragon.
The invisible light permeates winter's still point where darkness lingers through the mysterious female.

EARTHLY MOON CYCLE

The day after the dark moon is a time of renewal. This is the beginning of strength and hope. A point of light appears through a dark tunnel. Binary 1.

JUDGMENT

RETURN is a time wherein the union of the Tiger and Dragon in the RECEPTIVE changes into the APPROACH OF THE DRAGON. After this deep fusion similar to the winter solstice and the time of midnight, the APPROACH OF THE DRAGON is the arousal of the masculine principle. This is an opportunity to reawaken what has been asleep or hidden and to allow it free expression.

This is not a time to apply self-will, but to realize that the masculine forces are spontaneously emerging after a period of union. A sense of renewal is approaching and it is important for optimal growth that you have laid good foundations during quiet times. If your motivations have been in harmony with the Tao, a sense of revivication will now be yours. Keep your spirit free of corrupt motives and negative influences, and all obstacles to your most righteous aims will be overcome. Don't expect the future to be like the past.

MAN

For a man, RETURN is a time of the beginning with ascending renewed energy. Still it is not a time to exert oneself to the utmost. Rather, it is the inevitable return of the cycle in a new arc of awareness. Action will be spontaneous rather than forced. Like a coiled spring, RETURN is the beginning of the uncoiling or discharge of energy.

WOMAN

For a woman, RETURN is the epitome of psychic vision and intuitive seeing. It is a time when people of similar vision are united and can begin to work towards ideals envisioned. New activity will inevitably occur, but again there is no need to push or exert.

The situation will unfold by virtue of its own reserves of

energy. The end of a cycle has been reached now wherein intelligence has been coded in a seed of new beginnings. One need only plant the seed in virgin soil and it will grow of its own accord.

LINES

—X— 6 Great danger is present for you have missed the time to return to the right way. Do not insist on war or your own will for that will bring disaster.

—X— 5 By contemplating the situation and making a new start, your own faults will be overcome. Returning to righteousness will be beneficial.

—X— 4 Be independent if need be, but remain true to yourself above all, no matter what happens.

—X— 3 Vacillation of feelings and indecision are dangerous, but since you are generally sincere and of goodwill, your state of mind will improve.

—X— 2 Being inspired by the goodness and purity of others is very beneficial. Follow the best examples you know.

—O— 1 Do not consider desires which are contrary to your deepest truth about yourself. Use self-discipline and your character will strengthen.

 25 INNOCENCE

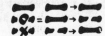

THE IMAGE

Streaming Jewels Explode into Lightning

The thighs of the Tiger moving through WIND ignite
FLAMES in the eyes of the Tiger.

Sincerity is spontaneous and true. The child of consciousness
acts from innate balance and can walk through fire.

HEAVENLY MOON CYCLE

Inner honesty is renewed by the unity of what one wants and what one is. Powerful moon elixir is the fulfillment through character development. Binary 57.

JUDGMENT

INNOCENCE is a time wherein the RETREAT OF THE TIGER is changing into the INNER TRUTH OF THE TIGER. This is a time to realize how everything in nature does what it must spontaneously. You need do nothing by will-power now. Rather, the will-less flow of the Tao can do all things through you.

This is a time to make silent and hidden the personality, so that the universal integrity within can do its work effortlessly. INNOCENCE is spontaneous integral oneness of individuality with the cosmic flow. There will be action by happening rather than effort. It is a refreshing time of innocent realization of the intrinsic action of things as they are. Everything has its own integrity which is its natural essence without imposed self-will.

MAN

For a man, INNOCENCE is a time wherein the inner vision of energy changing towards contemplation is becoming paramount. Now you see, spontaneously, how it is; and without effort the vision you see can be realized by the stimulation of self-evident truth.

As a man becomes more and more receptive, his energy rises into the heart where purification of all gross self-will is burned out. You can innocently and correctly realize your vision by standing aside and allowing your innate nature to speak.

WOMAN

For a woman, INNOCENCE is a time wherein the RETREAT OF THE TIGER as the feminine principle is activating her instinctual nature and rising up into her head as pure receptive intuition. From this open receptivity comes the vision to harvest whatever one has been working on. This harvest is not one's own; but is the harvest of the cosmic order.

You should not expect to be rewarded for your efforts now. Rather the efforts of manifestation are to be surrendered to the INNER TRUTH of the situation and thereby intrinsic rewards are found. The more the intrinsic rewards are realized in the heart of hearts, the more the harvest will be abundant for everyone concerned.

Honest motives result in spontaneous creative action and words.

LINES

—O— 6 Silence and stillness are necessary now. Integrity is presently maintained by no action at all.

—O— 5 Disease and shadowing influences will pass of themselves. Don't seek external remedies, for health will restore itself naturally.

—O— 4 Do not be impulsive now, but remain upright and maintain inner vision no matter what others may do or say.

—X— 3 Unexpected difficulties have come, but by maintaining your innocence and integrity, those who deviate from virtue will suffer.

—X— 2 If you have been diligent in your work and of upright intentions, you can reap a harvest. But stop dreaming of results. Live in the present moment.

—O— 1 With innocence and spontaneous goodness your aim will be reached.

26   FORCE OF GREAT

THE IMAGE

Reflecting Mountains Penetrate into White Light

The eye of the Tiger in the FLAMES of the galaxy spins into the LAKE reflected in the mouth of the Tiger.

The memory of the virtuous is stored in the words and deeds of history. The wise mother is firmly loving. The young and old trees are nourished by the same sun and earth.

HEAVENLY MOON CYCLE

The waning half moon brings interior nourishment from simple attention and integrity. To admit weaknesses is to have strengths. Binary 39.

JUDGMENT

In the FORCE OF THE GREAT, the INNER TRUTH OF THE TIGER becomes the POWER OF THE GREAT OF THE TIGER. The essence of the Tiger is in the heart. A storehouse of love and energy is accumulated in the heart. It is essential now to find the right distribution of this energy and to nourish humanity as a whole through whomever you meet.

The movement from the INNER TRUTH OF THE TIGER to the POWER OF THE GREAT OF THE TIGER is a powerful transition, for the accumulated energy is on all levels: physical, psychological and spiritual. Useful exchange is necessary at this time to allow the resources to nourish yourself and others. The POWER OF THE GREAT means to find the right expression or placement to build a joyous culture. This nourishment is to be placed according to the deepest heart's knowledge. This may be according to traditional values, but only if tradition is in accord with the cosmic laws. Then the stream of nourishment you find within yourself will be long lasting and of value to many.

MAN

For a man, this means the emanation of INNER TRUTH from the heart. The subtle current moves from there down the central channel to the base of the spine and up the back where the heart and throat chakras are rooted in the spine. Here the rising stream of creative energy awakens you. This is an opportunity to realign the direction of your activities to the cosmic order.

WOMAN

For a woman, the subtle current moves from the heart down the central channel to the base of the spine and up the back. She receives great intuition and vision in the head centers before the subtle current descends to the solar plexus center. Here there is a reservoir of potential energy for creative manifestation.

This transition is not only one of opening up nerve centers and becoming aware of the whole, but of having the power to distribute downward to others what was built up in reserves. You may now become a nourishing reservoir.

LINES

—O— 6 Because you have disciplined yourself in the past you now have great potential energy and reserves. It is now time to move ahead always acting in accordance with the cosmic order.

—X— 5 Don't confront your opponent, but instead restrain and redirect energy from destructive to constructive channels. Then good fortune will be yours.

—X— 4 Although you have been held back in the past, this has enabled you to accumulate reserves of energy that can now be used. Maintain righteous self-discipline and a balanced mind.

—O— 3 Train yourself to ask always what is right, be cautious and step by step you can now move forward.

—O— 2 Restrain yourself and cultivate centering so that when the right time comes, your resources of energy will be used beneficially.

—O— 1 Cease action and find peace in yourself. Don't waste energy by running around, but center in your deep self.

27 NOURISHMENT

THE IMAGE

Vast Seas of Mountains Condense into Lightning

The hands of the Dragon contemplate the vast MOUNTAINS whereby the THUNDEROUS feet of the Dragon are stilled.

Nourish all things without distinction. Being one with all things is giving to all things.

HEAVENLY MOON CYCLE

A pivot point of self-reflection, the moon elixir pervades the being of all sentience. Binary 33.

JUDGMENT

NOURISHMENT reveals the CONTEMPLATION OF THE DRAGON changing into the APPROACH OF THE DRAGON. This is a time of awareness of a complete mirroring of heaven and earth, of macrocosm and microcosm. It is a time to realize how everything is interdependent.

You are experiencing two contrasts. The CONTEMPLA-TION OF THE DRAGON is a tranquil awareness of vast orders of the cycles of life; whereas the APPROACH OF THE DRAGON is a shocking awareness of the unpredictable nature of events. This transformation of the masculine principle gives one an opportunity to observe polar extremes of energy within oneself. This will itself bring to bear the right proportion of nourishment, whether of food, impressions or friends.

MAN

For a man, NOURISHMENT is the relationship of the reservoir of contemplative energy to the release of that energy. It may be a time when relationships can take on a mutually nourishing character, but only if one has discipline over the thought patterns through the inner guidance of the heart. Outbursts of emotion are to be avoided by means of support and nurturing of others.

WOMAN

For a woman, NOURISHMENT is a time to realize the masculine principle within her as an open intuitive widening of perspective. This is expressed as a vision of what to take in to your system and what to reject. This rule applies to your nourishment and support of others as well.

A woman does well to be discriminating on the basis of wide and deep vision of the interrelationships of parts to wholes. The question to be asked is, 'What is the common good?' Anything excessive is to be avoided for balance is the keynote in NOURISHMENT.

LINES

—o— 6 You can now influence and nourish others and being conscious of the responsibilities, you can move forward and adversity will be overcome. All concerned will be nourished thereby.

—x— 5 Cultivate character and be satisfied with the rewards that have come to you. Don't attempt to help others if you lack the necessary strength now.

—x— 4 Great desires for nourishment should not lead to excess, but just the right measure. If you are in an influential position, enlist help to nourish others as well. Everyone will then benefit.

—x— 3 Temporary pleasures and values create disorder and eventually will bring about your downfall.

—x— 2 If you seek values and methods which are inappropriate to your own needs, you will lose your own nourishment and truth of self.

—o— 1 Don't seek the nourishment and prosperity of others or you will lose yourself. Remain simple and modest and give up envy.

THE IMAGE

Rainbow Sands Vaporize into Comets and Stars

The mouth of the Tiger roars beyond the LAKE as the thighs of the Tiger move on the WIND.
Standing alone with a shadow at the source brings extraordinary weight. Move lightly away.

EARTHLY MOON CYCLE

Intense introspection and withdrawal is brought through a self-reflective point. Too much anticipation brings anxiety and disappointment. Release what is clinging. Binary 30.

JUDGMENT

CRITICAL POINT is a change from the POWER OF THE GREAT OF THE TIGER into the RETREAT OF THE TIGER.

This is a time wherein restraint and building up potential has reached a limit. You are carrying more than you can bear and must find a way to become sensibly flexible again. Responsibilities, decisions and pressing business are all coming to a head. This is a critical time where you must become clear of what to do next and take action immediately. Your burdens are too heavy. Do not run away from the situation but sort out priorities according to a definite goal.

There may be conflict and chaos in the present situation. If so, regard it as an extreme dynamism and tension which can be creatively used towards balance by using your deepest calm mind. Reacting excessively to the situation is counter-productive. Find your own inner reserves and re-establish harmony as soon as possible through your own centered gentleness.

WOMAN

For a woman, CRITICAL POINT is a time wherein the accumulation of energy has been in restraint from doing anything or manifesting what she truly values. It is time to manifest, and to take action at this time is urgent. Strength and certainty within are essential to allow the reserves of energy to flow into the situation. The demands are great and it is imperative to renounce delay, excuses, procrastinations and falsehoods and get on with it.

MAN

For a man, CRITICAL POINT is a time wherein the responsibilities of his life must find priorities. The upper back and neck, where sometimes tensions accumulate, can become true strength rather than tension by becoming clear on value priorities. Use this time to determine exactly what to do according to cosmic law regardless of social influences. This takes courage according to clear vision.

LINES

—x— 6 Making great sacrifices is alright but realize what it costs to accomplish your purpose now.

—o— 5 The critical point has been reached where, if you attempt to build superstructures on rotten foundations, there will be a limited time of stability.

—o— 4 You have the strength to support the true purpose of the situation. Don't depend on externals but on your inner power.

—o— 3 There is danger in the excessive weight of the situation and nothing you can do will alter it now.

—o— 2 Even the old and withered, the modest and simple, can be revitalized by right organizations of the weak and old working on the outer, and the strong and young working on the inner sides of life.

—x— 1 Resilience is developed by being flexible under adversity. When beginning something, be cautious and adaptable.

29   ABYSMAL

THE IMAGE

Vast Seas of Sands Consense into Comets and Stars

The feet of the Dragon run downward on THUNDER as the MOUNTAIN rises out of the spread hands of the Dragon.

In the watery abyss spirit is returned to darkness where fluids force space into wholeness.

HEAVENLY MOON CYCLE

Watching oneself is within a self-reflecting pivot point of moon cycles. Deep introspection brings spontaneous movement. Binary 16.

JUDGMENT

ABYSMAL is the source of the dragon hexagram. It is the polarity of the APPROACH OF THE DRAGON transforming to the CONTEMPLATION OF THE DRAGON.

This is a time to be aware of danger, but as long as sincerity is present the great transformations occurring now will be fortuitous. Keep a steadiness of aim and flow with the currents. There is danger on all sides in your circumstances, but if you persist with integrity inwardly, the conditions will pass.

The present dangers are to be met openly and worked on with an uncompromising resolve to do what is right. The approach is to be direct and the contemplation to be all-pervading. There will be strengthening of character through repeated danger with this attitude.

WOMAN

For a woman, ABYSMAL is a time of great inner vision but difficult outward circumstances. This vision is necessary to carry you through the danger. Maintain your ideals and ethics and allow the currents that are happening now to descend of their own accord. By letting go of outward conditions and maintaining inner composure and consistent values, the creative power will rise, enabling you to realize more fully why things are as they are.

Your balance of mind amidst trials will convince others of the value of your vision. You can then move on to inspire others with values which can lead people out of the 'holes' they are stuck in. By example, you can be an inspiration amidst difficulties.

MAN

For a man, ABYSMAL is a time wherein effort must be applied to approach any existing problems with sincere commitment to work on them. Move forward actively until mastery is achieved. The signs of this are an inspirational rising out of the abyss of danger through an ongoing thoroughness. Then there will be penetration to the meaning of your present circumstance. This insight will liberate you from the danger. Accept and work with the difficulty and it will change into great inner resources which will free you.

LINES

—X— 6 Your own ignorance and stubbornness have sustained the danger and you are now irremediably caught. Nothing to do now but wait and reflect.

—O— 5 Dangers pass of their own accord if you dissolve ambitions and arrogance.

—X— 4 Be honest and sincere amidst difficulties and seek only clarity and equanimity. All pretense must be banished. It doesn't impress anyone.

—X— 3 Great danger is increased by lack of understanding. Be true to yourself and take no action.

—O— 2 Stay afloat of the tides of life's dangers by remaining calm and clear. Small efforts in a sea of adversity can help.

—X— 1 Don't overestimate your power now. There is extreme danger for you have lost sight of who you are in relation to others.

30   FLAMING BEAUTY

THE IMAGE

Rainbow Mountains Vaporize into Lightning

The thighs of the Tiger in moving with the WIND open into the LAKE reflected in the mouth of the Tiger.

In the clarity of fire, awareness between the eyes is focused to a single light wherein memory of the source is illumined.

HEAVENLY MOON CYCLE

Self-reflecting clarity of fire over fire brings timeless illumination repeating the intensity of the moon elixir. Binary 45.

JUDGMENT

FLAMING BEAUTY is the Tiger herself as a flaming synergy of forces. She is represented by both the RETREAT OF THE TIGER and the POWER OF THE GREAT OF THE TIGER as the dual aspects of silence and roar, of intuition and creativity, of receptive reflection and active penetration. This is a time for spreading light to the cosmic six directions through discriminating caution, intelligence and powerful spontaneous leaping into one's destiny.

MAN

For a man, FLAMING BEAUTY means the inner vision brought about by the subtle current which descends. When it rises into the central channel of heart and brain, it becomes a fiery furnace of energy whereby the subtle current descends to the base of the spine and up the back to the upper center of the back. The heart, aflame, can now speak out. The alignment of desire to the common purpose can bring greater clarity and enlightenment to those who follow. This is a time of both clarity and activity. Realize now what is true in the situation and act in harmony with the truth.

WOMAN

For a woman, FLAMING BEAUTY reveals the subtle current rising up the spine which brings inner receptivity and vision by her being completely open to the situation. Then, once the clarity of vision comes, it is time to take action as the subtle current comes into a desire for creative manifestation.

This release of energy for a woman is not merely undisciplined euphoria or dissipation, but a creative action with reserve and awareness. This is definitely a time to bring awareness to a head so that, by the interactions of ascending and descending energy, the whole is realized to be greater than the sum of the parts.

This is one pole of the Tantric union wherein the feminine principle is both quiet and evocative, both receptive and creative, both discriminating and illuminating.

LINES

—O— 6 Now is the time when you can overcome adversities by your penetrating clarity. After vanquishing confusion, create balanced moderation and all will be well.

—X— 5 True remorse for overly indulgent tendencies and sincere resolve to overcome these weaknesses will bring you many blessings.

—O— 4 Fast burning light consumes energy too quickly. Slow down or you will exhaust your reserves.

—O— 3 Make the best use of the propitious time, for rampant thoughts and feelings will restrict your mobility and the fullness of your life. Otherwise be happy.

—X— 2 Now is a beneficial time if you maintain your center and balance. Indulge in nothing and a warm beautiful yellow light will shine in your life.

—O— 1 Preparing to advance now has disorder and many new impressions, but if you keep your inner vision, there will be good fortune.

31 INFLUENCE

THE IMAGE

Rainbow Sands Evaporate into Coals of Fire

The ears of the Dragon hear the WATERS changing into the WIND where the Tiger rests on her thighs.

Mutual benefits of bees and flowers permeate the air. Influence is most pervading when inconspicuous.

EARTHLY MOON CYCLE

With the waning moon it is time to stimulate others in preparation for the new moon. All beings are drawn together by their innate nature. Binary 28.

JUDGMENT

INFLUENCE is the transformation of the HUMBLE VIGILANCE OF THE DRAGON into the RETREAT OF THE TIGER.

This is a time to contemplate the mutual resonances of the universe and most particularly the attraction of the sexes found throughout nature. Now you can become aware of the magnetism of all beings with affinities. Just as certain plants thrive only in certain soils and climates, so human beings also must realize where they are best able to function. This is a good time to free one's mind of attachments and to see the innate tendencies of all parties concerned.

At this time you may be deeply touched in heart and may also touch others deeply. Expressing mutual appreciation is beneficial to all concerned. Friends, family, community, business and all relations may be more open to influence now, so make sure of your own motivations and you will reap rewards accordingly.

During times when you easily attract others, discretion must be used. Even if others are won over by flattery or pressure, if you seek control according to selfish aims in the end it will be a waste of energy and time. Appreciate those around you for their own good and you will be benefitted also.

WOMAN

For a woman, INFLUENCE is an increasing knowing through the waves of subtle current. It is time now to have confidence that what the essences are telling you is true. Accept the natural attraction of the situation and free yourself of prejudice. It is time to allow mutual affinity to be the intelligence behind future moves. This is a beneficial time to marry for both man and woman.

MAN

For a man, INFLUENCE is a major transition and because of this the large cycles of things can be felt and seen at this time. Do not hesitate if you feel an irresistible magnetism or chemistry at work in a relationship. It is a profound attraction which is in harmony with cosmic law at this time.

LINES

—x— 6 Talking of ideas and values and desires is of no use unless action and sincerity are behind the words. Talk is only talk.

—o— 5 Although you want to influence others, the response is not there now for the aims are too shallow. No remorse.

—o— 4 Love and affection are growing deeply. Cease any manipulative attitudes and you will naturally know how to influence those dear to you. A common positive purpose is beneficial.

—o— 3 Don't be impulsive and impetuous or your actions will lead to humiliation. Develop self-control and anxieties will vanish.

—x— 2 You are still unaware of the direction of development in the present. Be vigilant and calm.

—x— 1 There is a light attraction occurring now but this is of little significance. Friendships develop naturally if you remain centered.

32 DURATION

THE IMAGE

Rainbow Caves and Valleys Evaporate into Comets and Stars

The mouth of the Tiger speaks in LAKES of WATERS rippling into the ears of the Dragon.

Gentleness and strength endure. When vibrations cease, there is recycling. Sun and moon follow each other continuously.

EARTHLY MOON CYCLE

To sustain abundance depends on perseverance and long-enduring values. Continue in one direction and fulfillment will be sustained. Binary 14.

JUDGMENT

DURATION is the POWER OF THE GREAT OF THE TIGER changing into the HUMBLE VIGILANCE OF THE DRAGON.

Although there may be obstacles in your path, you have the sustaining power to go through them now until your aim is reached. It is a time to realize the consistency in your life. Find out clearly what has had constancy of value for you in the past and use this as a power to continue in an unswerving direction for the future. This does not imply past events so much as your deepest values.

WOMAN

For a woman, DURATION is a time of great power to manifest long-term values without great effort. The cosmic flow is in favor of your actions, which are in accordance with the common good. Therefore you need not make a point or show of the power which is yours to use now. Just allow it to flow into directions which have been established by attunement to the cosmic order.

You will know this by your humble attentiveness to the needs of others. This will give the present currents of growth and creativity an appropriate vehicle. Do not cling to traditional values, but neither negate them if they are still of service to others. Then your power and creativity will have order and will endure.

MAN

For a man, DURATION is a time wherein great power is on the increase, enabling creative inspiration which is the fountainhead of your enduring aims at this time. Allow your character to be molded on the basis of your highest creative insights on the values relevant to you and your loved ones.

These values may be already in effect among those close to

you and your society. If so, then continue your support of policies or methods of allowing them to endure. In this way you can rest assured that the largest overview will be sustained also by your contemplations and receptive attitudes, which enable energy-fields to build and resonate. Sometimes the greatest things are accomplished by humble non-doing, but with an awakened vision. Obstacles are then removed not by force, but by a dissolving.

LINES

—x— 6 Indecisiveness and anxiety lead to confusion. Nothing can be accomplished with unrealistic aims. You will endure by the development of your wisdom and insight into the situation.

—x— 5 Use effort appropriate to the mundane and lofty aims, each according to its value. If you are a leader, be flexible; if you are a follower, be constant and true to your leader.

—ᴄ— 4 Cease wasting your energy on worthless aims. Reassess your values and find something realistic and worthwhile.

—ᴏ— 3 Inconsistency in yourself leads to loss and humiliation. You are unpredictable even to yourself which increases your difficulties.

—ᴏ— 2 A balanced right measure of effort with a right aim will be to the point.

—x— 1 Precipitous changes are not advantageous now. There is trouble in trying shortcuts or hasty results.

33 RETREAT

THE IMAGE

6 Rainbow Jewels Vaporize into Coals of Fire

The thighs of the Tiger balance all WIND into the stillness of the MOUNTAIN and night sky.

Withdrawing is as important as approaching. When the child is born, the mother can rest. Go within the petals of protection rooted in heaven.

HEAVENLY MOON CYCLE

Now is the time to go completely within and allow the moon elixir to pervade your being. Two days before full moon gives inner nourishment to sustain fasts and meditations. Binary 60.

JUDGMENT

THE RETREAT OF THE TIGER is one of the immutable golden hexagrams wherein you may find yourself quiet, aloof and hidden.

This is a time to withdraw from social and public affairs and detach yourself from any entanglements. The Tiger is silently waiting for prey while hidden in the grasses. It is best now to be anonymous or unseen.

There is no war to be fought now, nor struggle to carry on. Rather it is a time to cease communication and abandon everything that has demanded your intense attention. Absent yourself momentarily from involvements and, if need be, arrange for others to take your place.

The whole world may be at war, but it is not now your concern. Have confidence that to detach from all fears and desires is absolutely necessary now.

WOMAN

For a woman, it is a time to allow inner reserves to accumulate while doing nothing outwardly. Concern yourself with inner reinforcements and awarenesses which will become reserves to use when any conflict has ceased.

MAN

For a man, RETREAT manifests as clear vision. It is important to have perspective on the total situation and not see it only from one particular vantage. Become composed and equanimous, for taking the situation silently at this time is best for all concerned.

LINES

—o— 6 A difficult situation is falling away and by sustained retreat you will have freedom from it.

—o— 5 A firm withdrawal is beneficial by maintaining inner composure and outer flexibility.

—o— 4 Retreat and maintain inner purity with resolved discipline or you may suffer greatly from entanglements.

—o— 3 Inferior forces prevail around you. Retreat from inferior forces and resume personal interests.

—x— 2 Attune to inner guidance and be firm with yourself in aligning in a direction of truth. Then further confusion will be avoided.

—x— 1 Stay still. You have waited too long before retreating. There is great danger in going ahead now.

34 GREAT POWER

THE IMAGE

Rainbow Caves and Valleys Vaporize into White Light

The mouth of the Tiger speaks of all of heaven reflected in the LAKE.

The great within the depths of the lake is expanding to be born. Feminine power is in the womb of space and creative arts.

EARTHLY MOON CYCLE

Just before full moon is a moment when anything can be accomplished. Make sure your values are right and expand to fullness. Binary 15.

JUDGMENT

The POWER OF THE GREAT OF THE TIGER is one of the eight immutable golden hexagrams. Here you can test your true character, for everything you say or do will influence others . . . for good or ill. This is a time of great personal power and therefore a time of responsibility. Use this time with caution for all your goals must be honorable to pass this test.

This is a time of great power and therefore the correct use of this power is of paramount concern. Inherent rightness and relaxed naturalness are important when great force comes to the surface. If you want to learn something, be still and humble, for deep wisdom is itself the root of power.

The Taoist awareness of 'wu wei' (doing-by-non-doing) is the effortless power directed by virtue or the wisdom of the common good. Allow energy to gather to your true center and you will naturally know what to do.

MAN

For a man, the POWER OF THE GREAT OF THE TIGER is centred in the upper back up to the throat. This is a place of either great power or great tension. Tension indicates being insecure and is exceedingly dangerous now because of the power locked up inside the present situation. If you do not have such tension then rest assured that others look up to you now for an example of character and responsibility.

WOMAN

For a woman, the POWER OF THE GREAT OF THE TIGER is centered in the heart chakra. This is the greatest power there is in the world and, used well, can influence others to refine their characters. You may be the center of attention because of the magnetic power of the heart, which you can exercise now. Do not abuse this time by thinking such power is possessed by you. Rather it is a current influence which you can use to strengthen your character by having the strength and courage to love sincerely, even amidst great trials.

LINES

—✗— 6 Don't complicate matters by forcing yourself stubbornly, for in this way you can neither advance nor retreat. Compose yourself and the matter at hand will be resolved.

—✗— 5 Apply power to yourself in releasing rigid positions and don't attempt to prove yourself. The difficulty will dissolve of itself.

—O— 4 Use power appropriately at the right place and at the right time and obstacles will give way easily. Maintain inner directions of truth.

—O— 3 Don't demonstrate your power. Open display of strength is a weakness and will draw attack upon itself. Maintain inner calm and the strength will come of itself.

—O— 2 Moderation and caution are needed for your power may be too forceful for the situation.

—O— 1 Don't force the issue. You have great power, but to push ahead now will only lead to conflict.

35 PROGRESS

THE IMAGE

Streaming Mountains Explode into Coals of Fire

The thighs of the Tiger move on WIND as the belly of the dark EARTH opens to new growth.

The birth and flight of the butterfly is a surprise to those who know the caterpillar. Reach upward from a centered place in your being.

HEAVENLY MOON CYCLE

The bridge with the super-conscious is being made from the unconscious. Just after the waning half moon is a time of integrating aspirations. Binary 40.

JUDGMENT

PROGRESS is the RETREAT OF THE TIGER changing into the RECEPTIVE UNION OF THE TIGER AND DRAGON.

This is a time to discover the illumination within and move with it towards receiving many kinds of people. It is time for you to advise others according to your greatest virtue and illumination. Setting an example is the best way, but, in addition, communicating your insights will be beneficial to others just now.

Bring your greatest insights into the service of others by being receptive to their needs. Your counsel may take only a few words which strike at the heart of the situation. Your society or group has the potential of development through illumined leadership.

Do not be put off by the recognition you may receive now, but use this time to influence others only on the basis of the wisdom you have found in your retreats. Mutual support of leader and followers results in progress for all.

WOMAN

For a woman, PROGRESS is a time of purification. What is needed is to discipline yourself to find illumination within and let it emanate to others without deliberation. You are dependent on others for support of some kind and, by being a virtuous example while living with others, your influence will spread. Effort is needed only in purification processes, not in activities.

By realizing the illumination within you, and being receptive to how daily life situations actually are, you will have an effect on people. Strive for nothing but clarity. All else will come by itself.

MAN

For a man, PROGRESS is a time of great illuminative insight. This is not a time to take action so much as to bring this insight into the counsel of others. First you must become contemplative and then openly receptive to whatever problem arises within your group or society.

You may be honored with gifts. Accept them, but realize the source from which they came is not separate from yourself. Your prominence is to be used in service of others who have less vantage and vision at present. You have an opportunity to bring clarity into a maelstrom of different situations. Cling to nothing and consider the whole.

LINES

—o— 6 Don't go further now or you may have cause for regret. The situation is too ripe or expanded and needs limits and regulation. Alienation comes from forcing oneself on others.

—x— 5 Proceed in the right path and don't be concerned with loss or gain. Blessings are in store if you progress for truth alone.

—o— 4 There is progress but with inferior motives. This is a questionable advancement and dangerous. Stop and realign your aims with right motives and people.

—x— 3 Your intentions and actions are correct and consequently all involved have agreement and truth. Progress is made through trust.

—x— 2 There is difficulty. It is best not to worry about rapport with a feminine authority, for the worry hinders progress. Keep calm and centered.

—x— 1 Attend to your work with clear vision of the right path. Correct intentions must be backed by unswerving effort without thought of reward.

36 DARKENING LIGHT

THE IMAGE

Reflecting Caves and Valleys Penetrate into Lightning

The belly of the dark EARTH opens into the LAKE reflected in the mouth of the Tiger.

The butterfly does not show its wings when in the chrysalis, but the hidden transformations are great.

EARTHLY MOON CYCLE

Like the dark side of the moon, one shines although unseen.
The waxing moon is not always visible. Binary 5.

JUDGMENT

In DARKENING OF THE LIGHT we see the copulation of the
Tiger with the Dragon changing into the POWER OF THE
GREAT OF THE TIGER. This is a time wherein the negative
aspect of the receptive appears to be a 'dark night'. This is the
'luminous darkness' of deep awareness of unconscious forces.
The deepest levels of your being are awakening in the
DARKENING LIGHT, but they cannot be spoken about. This
is a time to allow your deep destiny to reveal itself and to
maintain a fierce inner vigilance without wavering. The time is
not easy, but it strengthens your character if you are true to
yourself at this time. Be willing to know the truth about
yourself and be honest.

MAN

For a man, the subtle current awakens in the sexual center in
the DARKENING LIGHT. This arousal will immediately rise
up into the central channel into the heart and brain where the
fires are purified. From the base of the spine the subtle current
rises up the spinal column to the upper back and throat.

This is not a time to act, but to simply be aware and know
your most deep tendencies for what they are. Any clinging,
greed, resentments and worry must be brought to the luminous
darkness where it becomes clear to you what needs to be
sacrificed. Do not speak or act, but allow the luminous
darkness to shine inwardly on all repressed tendencies.

WOMAN

For a woman, the subtle current of the DARKENING LIGHT
begins with her highest receptivity in the 'Jade Gate' in the back
of the head. The darkness is often a woman's native territory.
She can allow the darkness and the void to be acceptable at this
time. From such surrender comes vision and from thence an
awareness of subtle tendencies which have influenced her

actions in the past.

You can now become aware of past faults in action and word and bring them to consciousness, and eradicate them completely by simply bringing them into awareness. This is a formidable time, for it is not a time to do anything. Rather you can allow all your accumulated impurities to rise to the surface and examine them. By doing so they will dissolve of themselves.

LINES

6 A storm and darkness has overcome the situation. This is a time to lay low and not attempt to change anything. Storms don't last forever.

5 You are in the middle of a dangerous situation and it is best to remain outwardly flexible while maintaining your inner clarity and resolve for the truth.

4 Leave the situation at once for it has no hopes for you and you do well to preserve your own inner light and calmness of mind.

3 By steady unswerving directives toward overcoming your own inner darkness, outward circumstances will change to benefit all concerned.

2 You have suffered an injury, but this very injury can inspire you towards affirmative action if you maintain inner resolve for the common good.

1 Move on, for your environment is full of obstacles to your journey. Although your basic needs are met, your motives are not understood and if you try to impose yourself there will be hostility.

37   FAMILY

THE IMAGE

Reflecting Jewels Penetrate into Lightning

The hands of the Dragon contemplate the MOUNTAIN rising up to the pure white light of HEAVEN.

Words coming out of clarity are like wind out of fire. Each person's vibration contributes to the whole brightness.

HEAVENLY MOON CYCLE

Inner resonance is what draws each to each. The subtle moon elixir is so penetrating your being that others recognize it now. Binary 53.

JUDGMENT

In FAMILY we have the CONTEMPLATION OF THE DRAGON changing into the CREATIVE UNION OF THE TIGER AND DRAGON. This is a change wherein the masculine principle is quite still so that the virtues of faith, loyalty and obedience come to the fore and the different members of the family or group find their rightful places. This is not done by force, aggression or dominance, but by each member coming into inner accord with the other members, so that harmony exists without the dominance of a leader. Business, social systems or any other group endeavor should now be conducted by this inner contemplation wherein all force is set aside.

MAN

For a man, the etheric reservoir in the solar plexus center is replenished by your contemplation. By this process, CONTEMPLATION becomes creative ideas in your group. You may then communicate your ideas to find how they fit or transform the needs of the whole family.

WOMAN

For a woman, the etheric current of the CONTEMPLATING DRAGON is in the back of the spine. Your heart awareness is very central for the family or other group. As the current ascends from there, it becomes open intuition in the head and clear vision. Here you can see the harmony of all the members as a whole and energy for creative action in daily life is generated. At this stage it is well to communicate what needs to be done in daily life activities so that each family member understands his/her respective role.

LINES

6 Being faithful to the group and true to yourself is extremely beneficial, for unity of purpose brings unity of effort. There is mutual respect.

5 You can be open in relation to those who depend on you for love and guidance. Real security of a family or community brings happiness.

4 You can enrich others by furthering their growth through fulfilling duties with humble effort. This will recycle beneficially for all.

3 Keep balance and moderation in your relationships and there will be harmony. It is better to have discipline than self-indulgence.

2 You can give nourishment to the group without pushing ahead with inappropriate actions. Attend to simple matters at hand, one by one, for the benefit of all.

1 When relationships begin it is well to make clear the respective roles and maintain discipline, then there will be harmony.

38   OPPOSITION

THE IMAGE

Streaming Mountains Explode into White Light

The head of the white light of HEAVEN opposes the LIGHTNING *feet of the Dragon.*

That which rises too high cannot reflect in the lake below. Angular motions separate this from that in difficult dimensions.

HEAVENLY MOON CYCLE

The golden body is reaching its peak, nourished by the moon elixir; but self-defensiveness resists true release into spiritual power. Fear not the void for it is full. Binary 43.

JUDGMENT

OPPOSITION is the transformation of the solar nerve currents of the CREATIVE to the APPROACH OF THE DRAGON. This is a very electric and powerful situation wherein opposing outlooks are likely to be emphasized.

Contradictions cannot be overcome by force, but by understanding the nature of the opposing sides. There is a unity in the opposition but it cannot be exercised without realization of the inherent polarity of the situation.

The CREATIVE forces want to find expression, but cannot do so now directly. Rather they must be modified and ambitious goals stepped down so that there is no threat to others. Ideologies are divergent and one cannot proceed with the presence of misunderstanding. Rather, the opposing side must be accepted so that the whole is known and judgments and accusations put aside. Then what seemed like poison may be realized as medicine.

MAN

For a man, OPPOSITION is a time when creative ideas seek to be heard, but one's strongest ideals must be allowed to descend into the common reservoir of values. This is a descending subtle current down to the receptive sexual center and from there up into the central channel of abdomen and heart. From there the subtle current descends to the base of the spine.

The impetus to act for a man is now very powerful, but it is a time to use gentle influences to ease the opposition of ideas present.

WOMAN

For a woman, OPPOSITION is a time when the CREATIVE power of manifestation is strong, but instead of giving birth to creative activities of one's own tendencies, it is well to realize the opposing view. Otherwise there will be a clash in action.

The subtle current ascends from the sexual center into the central channel of abdomen and heart and down to the base of the spine, where it rises up the back over the head to the place of inner vision. It is at the place of vision that the action must be applied. There may be opposition among family members or those close to you, but the best procedure is to embrace all contradictions in one view of the whole.

LINES

—O— 6 You have lost perspective and a realistic comprehension of the situation due to suspicion. When this is dissolved, the relationship will flourish.

—X— 5 Although there has been estrangement, it is now a good time to have faith in the basic relationship and move ahead together, for all people concerned will benefit.

—O— 4 Difficulties and isolation exist, but if you hold inwardly to persons with whom you have an inner affinity there will be harmony and you can then work together.

—X— 3 Opposing force with force will only bring action to a halt. Difficulties are present which can only be overcome by adaptability and acceptance while being inwardly true to what you know is right.

—O— 2 Mutual attraction will benefit both a leader and subordinate even if the subordinate takes the initiative in communication.

—O— 1 Two strong forces are in opposition and there is estrangement. Don't seek to force a unity, for opposition implies an underlying unity and the situation will resolve itself naturally if you remain true to yourself.

≣≣ 39 *OBSTRUCTION*

THE IMAGE

Reflecting Sands Penetrate into Coals of Fire

The belly of the dark EARTH obstructs the path of motion by the thighs of the Tiger moving on the WIND.
Be still now and know that the unpassable abyss is a place to allow the inconceivable to be conceived.

EARTHLY MOON CYCLE

Now it is best to pause and wait, for a powerful insight is emerging with the waning of the moon. Binary 20.

JUDGMENT

OBSTRUCTION is the change from the RECEPTIVE UNION OF THE TIGER AND THE DRAGON into the RETREAT OF THE TIGER.

This time is difficult for it is nothing less than the movement from the state of union to a state of pause and retreat. The obstruction is internal and that is where to look for it. To blame others is completely inappropriate.

Persist in self-knowledge and the block to further union will be removed. It is time to hire or accept helpers or to serve others if they have a more clear vision than you do.

The best course is to be still and work inwardly on your own motivations and unbalanced tendencies. Gather energy rather than trying to push ahead, for expressed power now will only complicate your situation.

If there are difficulties in relationships, clear up your own side of the difficulty and remain as flexible as possible. Give up fighting now and cease struggle. The obstruction and opposition is a tension for growth. Why might you expect things to go according to any limited views you might have? Work hard on expanding your view and you may find the struggle has ceased.

WOMAN

For a woman, OBSTRUCTION is a time when intuition awakens but there are blocks to being able to manifest what you see. Energy is accumulated, but frustrations may exist. Realize that the source of the obstruction is possibly your own inner attitude. Overcoming any resentments, suspicions and doubts is essential. To do this character must be developed. This means using the energy that wants to indulge in selfish desire and turning it towards constructive contemplation of the right resources and the right aims. Choosing appropriate means is important now as well as the ability to join with others to realize common goals for humanity.

MAN

For a man, OBSTRUCTION is a time when sexual urges need
to be sublimated and brought into a love for all of humanity.
Then a clear vision of the future will appear spontaneously.
Keep positive thoughts and cease all possessiveness and
attachment. Then energies will be freed from their obstructions
and serve you to your highest destiny.

LINES

-X- 6 There are obstructions all around you which you
cannot avoid. Return to your true self, seek
guidance, and a wise leader will be found who can
help all concerned pass through the difficulties.

-O- 5 When obstructions are very desperate and great,
open honesty and true spirit will attract friends who
lead the way.

-X- 4 You cannot overcome the obstacle alone now. Be
open to others of like mind and allow the situation
to develop strength through united effort.

-O- 3 Return to your inner sense of truth and reconsider
what you are attempting to do. Going ahead now
meets with obstacles.

-X- 2 Serving a cause larger than yourself brings success
in overcoming extraordinary obstacles. Selfless
ministering leads to the dissolving of all misunderstandings.

-X- 1 Keep still in the face of obstacles and cease
seeking to take action. Wait and the right moment
to move will come of itself.

40 DELIVERANCE

THE IMAGE

Streaming Caves and Valleys Explode into Comets and Stars

The mouth of the Tiger is silent before the LAKE, delivering over the dark secrets of the belly of the EARTH.

The release of rain from clouds brings forgiveness to all parties. Gratitude brings you into the thunderous arms of the deep mother.

EARTHLY MOON CYCLE

The waxing moon brings spontaneous activity into new directions after tremendous build-up of tensions. In such deliverance who can blame others? Binary 10.

JUDGMENT

DELIVERANCE is the change from the POWER OF THE GREAT OF THE TIGER to the RECEPTIVE UNION OF THE TIGER AND DRAGON.

This is a time when danger is past, for great power has been expressed and is transforming the situation. Obstacles and difficulties are being resolved, but how they are resolved depends on how you take action and manifest the power available to you now. Above all, don't ruminate on the faults and misdeeds of others and begrudge old wounds inflicted on you. Give up and release this whole pattern and forgive others. Then be grateful for the abundance of opportunities available to you now.

This very stimulating time must be used to wash away impurities and receive new vigor to achieve new growth in your life. Return to your normal life with refreshed insights or else hasten to make the necessary vigorous changes.

WOMAN

For a woman, DELIVERANCE is a time when action should be taken to manifest what has been accumulating for a long time. Don't hesitate to be creative. This will liberate you from tensions which have been building and enable you to work inwardly towards harmonizing the situation after action is taken.

When you release the accumulated power, it may be stormy for a while, but this is a natural and spontaneous creative process at this time. After the storm is past, use this time in an intuitive communion with the sources of power. The power is not yours, but runs through you. Being grateful for the origins of creative power is a source of meditative nourishment which will renew all your relationships.

Resolution comes from dissolving hurts and resentments in the living waters of gratitude. This alone will carry you to the source of power and renew your ability to create for the future.

MAN

For a man, DELIVERANCE is a time of great initial effort and succeeding contemplation and receptivity. Like a thunderclap, you can now bring problems into the open and relieve tensions which have accumulated in the past. Allow the power you feel to become expressed creatively and then bring the situation into a happy communion between disparate factors.

After expressing the difficulties of the past, realize that now is a totally new opportunity. Be open to it and allow yourself to become receptive rather than active.

LINES

—X— 6 A forceful deliverance is called for now. The peak of energy is past and you can now continue with your work and help others along the way.

—X— 5 Negative forces will recede of themselves by your faithfulness to what is right.

—O— 4 There are people of inferior motives attached to you, but you can liberate yourself from this entanglement by being faithful to your highest ideals and openly upholding them.

—X— 3 Now that you have some power, the temptation is to be greedy and arrogant, but this is repelling to others who might otherwise help you. The danger now is that they will usurp your place.

—O— 2 There are inferior forces at work and to be delivered of them you must be particularly honest, straightforward and virtuous.

—X— 1 The way has cleared and you can consolidate your position and then take action holding to what is right.

41 DECREASE

THE IMAGE

Vast Seas of Mountains Condense into White Light

The eyes of the Tiger bring FLAMES through the heart into the running feet of the THUNDEROUS Dragon.

Make an offering of the lower for the higher and strengthen the weak. Tame the beast and encourage the timid.

HEAVENLY MOON CYCLE

The waning moon enables a deep plunge into the unconscious where conscious control is no longer needed. Diminish strength and the small will become large. Binary 35.

JUDGMENT

In DECREASE the INNER TRUTH OF THE TIGER transforms into the APPROACH OF THE DRAGON. This is a time to apply energy to simplification of life according to the INNER TRUTH of what one has seen. This is a time of sacrifice and offering and if one does it willingly, then nothing will be taken. It is a time to realize what is irrelevant according to the heartfelt truth of the matter and to approach the situation with complete acceptance.

MAN

For a man, DECREASE may indicate a decline of money, resources, energy, accomplices or any other 'currency'. But this very decline is the beginning of a new ascent. Therefore you do well to remain aware that the life-force which descends will also rise. At this time one best allows the time to pass without giving vent to passionate desire or expressing indignation, anger or hurt. The decrease is real, but clinging to it is a greater loss.

Applying energy to simplification is appropriate. This leads to integrity and character development.

WOMAN

For a woman, DECREASE is not only the descent of resources, but an increase of intuition. A woman does best at this time to let go completely of whatever she is clinging on to . . . for it is a time of surrender, openness and emptiness. Such openness leads to complete atunement to the cosmic order which reveals itself as intuition.

It is not yet time for taking action, but this gives a woman a quiescent awareness, amidst tangible losses of energy and resources, to prepare for action. The insight of the heart has moved here to the insight of the inner eye. It is beneficial to be reassuring to those close by and those dependent in any way on you.

LINES

—o— 6 Helping others and seeing a more universal vision will give you renewed energy to fulfill what is needed now. Serving others will bring a beneficial social position.

—x— 5 It is your destiny to be in the beneficial situation you now find yourself in. You are a recipient of protection and blessings from above.

—x— 4 Now that you see your difficulties you can correct the situation. Work now to solve problems and the right helpers and resources will come to you and wounds will be healed.

—x— 3 The focus of energy and attention is best maintained by two people, not three or one. Too many people or directions are unfocused now. A single point of view will attract a dialogue.

—o— 2 Maintain your position and energy. Do not sacrifice anything nor expect anything, but just accept things as they are for now.

—o— 1 Moderation in giving or receiving help is in accord with the times. Relinquish selfish motives and be a true friend.

42 INCREASE

THE IMAGE

Vast Seas of Jewels Condense into Lightning

The hands of the Dragon contemplate the MOUNTAIN rising into FLAMES reflected in the eyes of the Tiger.

The offering is received and movement becomes stable. When those above dispense to those below docility supports growth.

HEAVENLY MOON CYCLE

The penetration of the moon elixir is increasing with the waxing moon. Movement in any direction brings renewal. Binary 49.

JUDGMENT

INCREASE is the CONTEMPLATION OF THE DRAGON changing into the INNER TRUTH OF THE TIGER. This is a time of increasing energy and difficult things can be done with such energy. The intensity of the forces at this time comes from the CONTEMPLATION OF THE DRAGON which creates an energy-field which can overcome obstacles.

The awareness and insight of the forces at this time comes from the INNER TRUTH OF THE TIGER in the heart. The two combined create conditions for benevolent action.

MAN

For a man, the subtle current moves from the solar plexus center, where great reserves of energy are stored, down to the sexual center and up into the central channel to the heart.

In the heart is the cauldron, the chalice of light and awareness whereby all ways are opened to direct awareness and generosity is a natural flow of energy.

One can make sacrifices at this time for those in a less beneficial position, which will increase your worth in other's eyes. Others will consequently give you loyalty and there will be unity in the group or community.

WOMAN

For a woman, the subtle current is centered in the middle of the back and rises up the spine over the head and down to the sexual center. From there, it rises into the heart. This is a much greater change for a woman than for a man, for she must discard preconceived self-images or images of others and allow intuition to bring forth a vision of the situation spontaneously.

From this a woman receives great reserves of energy and finally realizes how she can be of service to others in the situation. From her heart comes essential goodness and this creates confidence in the hearts of others.

If there have been errors in the past, she can see them clearly now and sacrifice them without hesitation. Transformation by giving is appropriate now.

LINES

—O— 6 Don't cease giving to others and increasing their welfare. You will lose respect if you waver in your decision to benefit others.

—O— 5 Sincere kindness and actions which are to the benefit of all reveal your virtue and accomplishments.

—X— 4 By benefitting others you will help yourself. Express truth in words and actions and your advice will be followed.

—X— 3 Sometimes hardship comes which, if you keep to what is right, can greatly benefit you. Others will trust you all the more if you are trustworthy in difficulty.

—X— 2 Your good fortune comes from without as a result of your dedication to what is right. Maintain the flow of your daily life in a spirit of open cooperation.

—O— 1 This is a good time to undertake a large task. If you have the welfare of all under consideration, there will be great cooperating energy and good fortune.

43 RESOLUTENESS

THE IMAGE

Rainbow Sands Vaporize into White Light

The mouth of the Tiger speaks through the LAKE reflecting pure white light of HEAVEN.

Deciding to come into being is the issue of time. Fill empty vessels with precious fluids and your time will come.

EARTHLY MOON CYCLE

Just before dark moon is a point of great determination to accomplish the new. Great vision is born out of the abyss. Binary 31.

JUDGMENT

RESOLUTENESS is the POWER OF THE GREAT OF THE TIGER as the fire of the blood changing into pure yang light of the CREATIVE. It is a time to bring everything into the open and the light of day. There is a danger of using force. To do so will weaken your position. Instead you should use faith to find the truth of the matter.

After you make a firm decision, it is well to continue in a sustained direction to overcome all obstacles to your highest aim. Caution combined with resolute strength is appropriate now. Seek a balanced attitude, organize your resources and your aim can be achieved.

The only danger is to focus overly on the problem or to use unbalanced force. Tension is natural in the situation, but that is no excuse for recklessness. Virtue combined with clarity will eliminate the pressures and tensions in preparation for new energies. Be firm in decision once you see it.

MAN

For a man, RESOLUTENESS is in the spinal chakra at the back of the throat, connected with the thyroid gland. The resolve is an ascending current of the fiery female principle in the spine rising to the vibratory frequency wherein one has become resolved on the matter at hand and can voice it clearly to people concerned.

For a man it is best at this time to let whatever is changing to be known and make clear one's intention. There is danger in the frank openness of voicing the new resolve, but this danger is overcome because of the truth of the matter. It is not a time to compromise even one iota, but to announce honestly the uncompromising nature of the issue.

WOMAN

For a woman, RESOLUTENESS is the change of current from the spleen center down to the sexual center. This is a time towards clear creative manifestation. It is a time to release to the public the accumulated information and works of art or service which have been building within. It is important for you to distribute whatever wealth or resources, teaching or nourishment has come to you in accordance with what you know as true in your heart. It is a time of strengthening bonds by fruitful dispensations in harmony with heaven.

LINES

6 You are helpless when the seeds of delusion are within you and dangerous negative forces appear sweet. Look behind the lure of what you want and recognize things for what they are.

5 Now is the time to make firm resolutions and decisions. There are powerful difficulties rooted deep in the past which must be uprooted and eradicated completely.

4 Hesitation in the midst of danger cannot resolve difficulties as long as you won't listen or follow others' advice. Your lack of courage and resolution in this matter will only continue the obstacles.

3 The struggle is difficult as enemies are strong, but as you merge with the problem the situation will begin to turn for the better if you keep fortitude.

2 Intense vigilance is needed to be aware of a possible surprise difficulty. Keep guard, caution and inner resolve.

1 Don't attempt to push ahead now, for the obstacle cannot be overcome without cooperation. Abortive resolution is dangerous. Reconsider.

44 ENCOUNTERING

THE IMAGE

Rainbow Jewels Vaporize into Comets and Stars

The head of the white light of HEAVEN meets the thighs of the Tiger riding on the dark WIND.

You can lose your place by keeping it. Temptations of the flesh burn in invisible places.

HEAVENLY MOON CYCLE

The full moon brings the invisible radiance of the moon elixir
into the whole body. Plant seeds of values for autumn comes
after summer. Binary 62.

JUDGMENT

ENCOUNTERING is the transformation of the CREATIVE
UNION OF THE TIGER AND DRAGON into the RETREAT
OF THE TIGER.

This is a time when you are tempted to go beyond the climax
of the situation and seek to continue it. It cannot be done. It is
a dangerous time and it is best to retreat or return to a
disciplined routine.

Instead of indulgences it is a time to purify and realign
yourself with your highest destiny. Inferior elements abound
just when you have reached a peak of happiness and pleasure.
It is advised not to give in to such inferior elements, but to
speak openly the truth.

You may still have some negative tendencies which need to
be watched at this time. It is a good time to nurture both
yourself and others, and being aware of limitations and modest
energies or resources is a good way to develop now. The tasks
at hand may be larger than your means, so work on anything
you have neglected rather than seek to expand.

WOMAN

For a woman, ENCOUNTERING is a time wherein sexual
energy may be aroused. Chaos may come if she seeks to
continue the excitement instead of allowing the subtle energy to
move up into the heart and brain centers of the deep
unconscious. It is in the heart of hearts that true love is born
and the energy from pure love can permeate the body.

ENCOUNTERING is a time for a woman to keep a clear
check on temptations of a sexual or possessive nature by allowing the fire of the Tiger to dissolve any manipulative or reactive
qualities. Whether seeking to manipulate money, business,
husband, or friends, it is a time to retreat from such action and
examine your deepest values. Also do not be tempted by offers
which in any way deviate from your deepest values.

MAN

For a man, ENCOUNTERING is a time wherein creative ideas are particularly strong. It is important at this time not to get carried away by delusional ideals or far-fetched plans. Rather, it is a time to see clearly the truth of the situation and to drive away all temptations of grandeur with sensible statements of fact.

LINES

6 Independence and aloofness are all right now, but there is danger that you will become narrow-minded and lose cooperation with other people. This self-interest will confine you.

5 Although there are negative forces present, they need not bother nor deter you from your unshaken direction, which is in accord with cosmic law.

4 Don't be an elitist and separate yourself from people of lesser stature and circumstance than yourself. You are living in delusion. Wake up or there is great danger.

3 Neither danger nor error exists for the connection is not yet strong. Use this time to reflect on the situation and become clear so that when it is time to go ahead you will not be uncertain.

2 There is competition now which can be controlled by firm gentleness. If weaknesses show, others may overpower you. Keep quiet and it will be well.

1 The present opportunities may seem propitious, but there is an inferior quality in them which you should recognize. It is best to stop and not allow the situation to develop. Otherwise there is trouble.

45 GATHERING TOGETHER

THE IMAGE

Streaming Sands Explode into Coals of Fire

The ears of the Dragon listen to the rushing WATERS of vibration while the hands of the Dragon move together in contemplation of the MOUNTAIN.

The fruits of the harvest are easily gathered, when ripe. Trees fully laden spring up when fruits are plucked.

EARTHLY MOON CYCLE

During the waning half moon the inner principles of things gather like the sap of trees. After inhaling, exhaling is easy. Binary 24.

JUDGMENT

GATHERING TOGETHER is the HUMBLE VIGILANCE OF THE DRAGON changing into the CONTEMPLATION OF THE DRAGON.

This is a time of collecting resources, people and currencies to bring about a contemplation in community. This takes great humility and awakening among all people involved. A center of communal services can be developed now if you persist in an integrative spiritual development. Offer services to others and inspire them to strengthen their character and skills.

This preparation will be needed later when it will be tried and tested by the needs of humanity. Foreseen is forearmed and you can now prepare for more difficult times by bringing together collectives and reserves of all kinds.

WOMAN

For a woman, GATHERING TOGETHER is a time of great change whereby attunement to harmony or disharmony among family or community is paramount. Vigilance and keen perception of the present situation will lead to the correct relationship whereby assembling for a great undertaking can happen. Your ability to be intuitive without selfish desires will assist in the uniting power needed to create the harmony you envision among groups and collectivities.

Accept any confusion you feel as part of the process, allowing contemplation to lead to intuition.

MAN

For a man, GATHERING TOGETHER is a time wherein the lower energies within himself need to be drawn upward by means of attentive watching of irresolute desires. Initially this may be a humbling experience, but as you persist in witnessing yourself truthfully, a creative energy will mount which can inspire you to lead others into rejuvenating activities.

Use this time to know yourself through working with people towards a common aim of spiritual value. This may mean an alternation of inner contemplation with outward expression of the common objectives.

LINES

—x—   6 If you are selfish in your intentions there will be frustration, for a real spiritual gathering is only possible with selflessness.

—o—   5 Be sure of the correctness and virtuous qualities of leadership towards a common purpose and then your power and position will be justified.

—o—   4 Be courageous and generous in interaction with the group and the whole gathering will lead to success.

—x—   3 Cease being aggressive in attempting to join with a group you are attracted to. Move ahead in friendly alliance with someone in the group, but avoid single-handed independence.

—x—   2 Offer something for the spiritual purpose of the group for there is a sincere gathering together which will benefit all concerned.

—x—   1 Seek to understand the purpose of gathering so that your hesitation may come to an end. Look into the center of your being and find the clarity needed for a happy gathering.

THE IMAGE

Reflecting Caves and Valleys Penetrate into Comets and Stars

The feet of the Dragon run on THUNDER rising up to meet the WATERS rushing into the ears of the Dragon.

Old trees give forth new shoots and children grow under the loving eye of mothers with gentle penetration.

EARTHLY MOON CYCLE

Nearly full moon is a time to take pride in what is being accomplished and continue the effort. Binary 6.

JUDGMENT

In PUSHING UPWARD the APPROACH OF THE DRAGON transforms into the HUMBLE VIGILANCE OF THE DRAGON.

This is a time to make energetic progress towards an inner awakening. Will-power must be used to make the approach successful. Take initiative and have the courage to see people in authority you would not ordinarily see. This is in order for you to assess your resources and activate those which resonate with your highest goals. Well spent, reserves of either money or energy will regenerate. Don't hesitate to spend time with and communicate openly with either those above you or your nearest loved ones. All will benefit by your efforts and this will recirculate resources for your future use.

WOMAN

For a woman, PUSHING UPWARD is a clear state of vision or knowing which will turn effortlessly into action. All effort must be applied only to clarity of insight, then the course of events will unfold of its own accord. There is a release of energy around the head and eyes now and the result is an understanding of some aspect of the true order of the cosmos. You can see your relationship to others both above and below you and spontaneously this will give you the energy to take action.

You can be very creative in this way, manifesting effective results in institutions and communities, making policies and creative solutions which will be of genuine service to others. This will give you recognition such as you have never had and it is well to remain humbly aware that this is your destiny in the world.

The flow of the Tao works through those who do not block the energy by selfish aggrandizements. Accept your new recognition as just another ripple in the cosmic river.

MAN

For a man, PUSHING UPWARD is a time to apply will and energy to enable currents to rise into a new elevation of development. This will give you power unknown before and you will be in the limelight if this power is used for creative ideas useful to humanity.

Remain flexible with the clear intention of reaching your goal. Then you can see clearly from within how the cycle of renewal is in motion and you can contemplate the effects of your creative inspiration. In time, it is well to become completely receptive to the effects of your own efforts, which will enable them to flow forth into appropriate channels.

Your influence will be greatest after the initial effort, which is an approach to higher stations than you heretofore have known. Remain humbly attentive to all details as the new cycle begins.

LINES

6 Be steadfast and thorough in your work, for this is not a time of rising position and growth but of consolidation. Assess yourself not only with mental but intuitive evolutions of broad import, or there is danger of stagnation.

5 Allow your achievements to accumulate in gradual steps and don't allow your newly gained successes to lead to heedless conduct. Be thorough with your work.

4 Your promotion to higher status is very beneficial at this time. Maintain gentleness and rightness and your offering will be welcome and your truest purpose amplified.

3 Easy rising upward sometimes leads to nothing. Some doubt and constraints are needed to keep the easy ascent in balance.

2 Modest resources do not limit you if you are sincere and make an offering towards your highest destiny. Though you are young in this endeavor your sincerity will enable you to rise.

—x— 1 Though your present position is · low, your superiors approve of your rising position. If you work hard in your new opportunities, this will create greater confidence.

47 OPPRESSION

THE IMAGE

Streaming Sands Explode into Comets and Stars

The mount of the Tiger speaks through the LAKE reflecting
the MOUNTAIN embraced by the hands of the Dragon.

When passions are still, the corporeal soul is conquered. The
downtrodden rely on nothing but inner virtue and this
conquers all else.

EARTHLY MOON CYCLE

Without adversity, how could there be deep insight? As the moon continues to wane, it is well to go deeply within the silence. Binary 26.

JUDGMENT

OPPRESSION is the total transformation of the opposites of the POWER OF THE GREAT OF THE TIGER into the CONTEMPLATION OF THE DRAGON.

This is a time when reserves of energy have been or are being spent, but this very emptying is a situation whereby a renewal can take place. Take courage at this time when all support seems to have given way. This is a time to test your resourcefulness, your steadfastness and balance in the midst of trials. Endurance and strength of character are needed, but not shown through outward expression. Rather, this is a time to use your reserves of inner power and to keep silent.

WOMAN

For a woman, OPPRESSION can be extremely frustrating, for she has great energy which is held in check by events. If you seem to be moving backwards, this is only temporary, for your personal power must be relinquished so that cosmic and human values can rise within you more strongly. The advantage of adversity is that it can drive you more inwardly to your true purpose in life.

Persevere in pursuits in harmony with your deepest values and bring them into a clear contemplation. Your inner development can be greatly enhanced at this time. It is a time when manifesting power and speaking in the open is useless. Work instead on allowing creative unconscious tendencies to rise into contemplation. If groups or relationships are strained, commit yourself to whatever is to the common good and trust that the contemplative power of your mind (heart) will influence the situation to everyone's benefit. The results will only be known later. This is a test of faith, not delusion.

MAN

For a man, OPPRESSION is a time when will-power can be used beneficially by remaining inwardly calm while outward circumstances are either adverse or catastrophic. Allow your power to become creative inspiration for future use even though nothing can be beneficially expressed now. If you attempt to convince others at this time you will meet with frustration.

You can be a fountain of inspiration at this time, but are being held back by people and events around you. Allow this inspiration to become an enduring vision to further the rightness for which you stand. Do not communicate the vision now and do not let it become polluted or weakened by the outward circumstances. Contemplation of the vision will give you reserves of energy which can be used when the times are more favorable for open exchanges.

LINES

—x— 6 Arrogance or self-opinionated positions only lead to oppression. Change your attitude and the bondage will change to freedom and good fortune.

—o— 5 Your kindness and gentleness are sometimes taken advantage of, but if you maintain composure and steadiness the distress and adversity will change.

—o— 4 Good intentions must be backed by ability and action or there will be set-backs. In the end it will be well if you practice patience.

—x— 3 Ignorance and delusion about the reality of your situation and relations creates isolation. Calm yourself and allow priorities to appear.

—o— 2 You have had advantages and honor, but have not fully appreciated it. Indulgence and taking things for granted leads to adversity. Be self-aware and able to decline favors if they interfere with steady rightness.

—x— 1 Your fears and desires trap you and, until you become clear on how the adversity came about, there will be continued frustration. Be calm and open up to the truth of the matter.

48 THE WELL

THE IMAGE

Reflecting Sands Penetrate into Comets and Stars

The feet of the Dragon electrify the WATERS speeded by the WIND enveloping the thighs of the Tiger.

When the body is still, the generative force is stable and moves upward. Plants draw sap upward by the force of the sun. Rising fluid forces are powerful through the sinking waters.

EARTHLY MOON CYCLE

The light of the moon is inexhaustible, just as a well is. Deep well-springs of nourishment are beneath the dryest of deserts. Binary 22.

JUDGMENT

A WELL is the transformation of the APPROACH OF THE DRAGON to the RETREAT OF THE TIGER.

This is one of the totally changing golden hexagrams. A WELL represents a deep source of inexhaustible powers to use for transformation according to the needs of people around you. Humanity contains all types and the WELL nourishes them all. This is a time to realize common values of society according to inherent characteristics of humanity. There is an organic order of qualitative types like many rays within a circle or differentiation within the whole. This is a time of reaching to the source and thereby finding cooperation of the many to the common values in life.

THE WELL represents a time of possible reaching for immutable qualities in the very foundations of life. Examine what is constant in your life and what is changing and find ways to remain constantly profound while all the vicissitudes of life move around you. Your potential mental clarity is great and to reach it is to allow your thoughts to become still so that the spiritual power of the Tao can work deep within you.

WOMAN

For a woman, WELL is a time to realize the depth of the situation and allow universal truths to surface so that all can share in a greater awareness. Vision must here become reality through the fountain of inspiration in the deepest recesses of your being. Uncovering this well-spring will bring nourishment and recognition to many and you yourself may become a source of deep human values and wisdom.

MAN

For a man, WELL is a time wherein inspiration and ideas are flowing freely and one can store reserves of energy in the solar plexus through such creativity. It is important now to realize the deep well-springs of life common to all and thereby nourish individuals in their uniqueness. All the differences can be harmonized by deep insight and acceptance of each as they are.

LINES

—x— 6 Replenishment of resources is a sign of bountiful regenerative capacities and open-minded attunement to sources of nourishment. Your dispensing to others is very beneficial.

—o— 5 Your insight and wisdom are a source of nourishment to all around you. Continue your exemplary conduct.

—x— 4 Self-discipline is needed to purify your intentions and re-evaluate your goals. You have much to offer, but before making your offering, orderly reorganization of your life is necessary.

—o— 3 You have plunged to some depths of your psyche and purified yourself, but it is not yet time for others to recognize your true value. You are ignored for now.

—o— 2 Your aspirations are right but you may not be using your potential abilities or the wisdom of life presented to you. Work on yourself to reach the depth of yourself whereby you can grow.

—x— 1 The mud at the bottom of the well is not nourishing to drink but may be useful for growing lotuses. Acknowledge and work through your sullied thoughts and patterns of behavior to emerge into more purified states later.

49 REVOLUTION

THE IMAGE

Rainbow Sands Vaporize into Lightning

The ears of the Dragon hear the cycles of WATERS and waves rushing into pure white light of HEAVEN.

The eye of the vortex of whirling waters sees change from a still center. Fire and water separate in order to unite.

EARTHLY MOON CYCLE

Approaching the dark moon a polarity creates circles in the air. Begin from the center and allow opposites to circulate to a natural end. Binary 29.

JUDGMENT

REVOLUTION is the HUMBLE VIGILANCE OF THE DRAGON changing into the COPULATION OF THE TIGER AND DRAGON in the CREATIVE. This is a highly dynamic change. For there to become a CREATIVE outcome is a major transition from deep unconscious processes of both desires and ideas.

This is nothing less than bringing the unconscious into consciousness. It is best now to realize that a major REVOLUTION or reversal of the situation is necessary and not to hold back. It is more like an inside-out of the entire situation ... whether it be a relationship, a position, a transaction or a social unit.

At this time, it is well to be aware that the change is so drastic and refreshing that it will take time for the external aspects of your previous daily life to be transformed in accordance with the inner change. This is to be expected. But it is well to make changes in the environment and way of life as soon as possible so that the metamorphosis of the Dragon will bring renewal in daily life.

You can expect great movement now. Ride the current of momentum, but remember the direction of change. Everything moves in cycles, but the direction of growth and awakening depends upon your inner vigilance in the midst of conditions. Release the old and strive towards that which is a nourishing flame of the spirit.

MAN

For a man, the subtle current becomes totally CREATIVE when all the unconscious contents have become conscious and brought into the light of day. This is a time to bring everything into accord with the deepest revolution of your unconscious mind.

WOMAN

For a woman it is a profound change and you may feel 'in the dark' during this ascent of the subtle current. As you continue silent and open meditation, you will have a clear vision of what to do. Removing all irrelevant aspects of your life in accord with this vision is the first stage of your creativity. It is clearly a time to manifest total changes in your outer life in accord with your new vision.

A woman should find a way to convey the vision to others so that all relevant to the situation may take a creative action together. REVOLUTION is a more complete change for a woman than for a man.

LINES

—x— 6 Both the inner and outer changes are accomplished now. Consolidate the changes by working on details, not major revolutions. The new order is already established.

—o— 5 Great revolutions are outcomes of deep intuition put into effect. This timely change will benefit all, for your intentions and abilities are in accord with the cosmic order.

—o— 4 Only by careful reform of your ideals in accordance with cosmic law will you be able to serve people. Harmonious change is promised at this time.

—o— 3 Alternating aggressiveness and hesitation in changing your life leads to recklessness. Stop and make reforms step by step so that others can trust your reliability.

—x— 2 Transformation is timely now. Proceed to revolutionize your life with a vision to broad ideals.

—o— 1 Be still until you know the direction for right action. Gather energy for reforming past mistakes.

50 CALDRON

THE IMAGE

Rainbow Mountains Evaporate into Comets and Stars

The head of the white light of HEAVEN shines down upon the ears of the Dragon coiled in the WATERS of sacrifice.

Purification by fire is either voluntary or involuntary: a distilled offering. A celebration of acceptance.

HEAVENLY MOON CYCLE

All that one is comes from the cosmic sources. To recognize and reciprocate the day before the full moon is to offer one's inner being as a gift. Binary 46.

JUDGMENT

The CAULDRON is the transformation of the CREATIVE UNION OF THE TIGER AND DRAGON into the HUMBLE VIGILANCE OF THE DRAGON.

When the power of the CREATIVE is brought into alignment with humble acceptance of the divine will, there is true attunement with the cosmic order.

This is a time to trust in your highest will aligned to Tao and surrender completely to that, then clarity will come through humility. Your destiny is written in the 'heavens', and now is a time to realize more clearly what it is and give up all extraneous goals and values which are not in alignment with your truest destiny.

WOMAN

For a woman, now is a time of great creative manifestation. Others will know you by the cosmic outpourings in your activities. Allow all your actions to be in harmony with the cosmic order and you will have unfathomable power come through you. This power must not be personalized, but seen as the universal current that it is. Then it can be directed into channels of unlimited utility.

Many of the processes may be unconscious to you now, but it is valuable at this time to awaken so that what actions you perform will be in harmony with the common good. This is not a compromise, but an out-and-out sacrifice of personal attachments for the spiritual realization of your destiny in relation to the cosmic order. Accept both your creativeness and your humility.

MAN

For a man, the CAULDRON is a time wherein the highest creative inspirations can be expressed and it will be accepted by others. There is a fountain of spiritual insight possible for you at this time. After it is expressed to those near you, it is well to remain quiet and harmonize your aims with others. An acceptance of destiny is necessary to be able to contemplate the right strategies for attaining the goals of all concerned.

Finally, it is well to remain completely receptive and open to possibilities you never imagined, which may come as spontaneous intuitive flashes or from others. Then, through your own humble awareness, you will know how to flow with the cosmic currents as they come.

LINES

6 Moderation and a balanced offering are very successful now. Your integrity is known and people around you are nourished by wisdom and good-will.

5 Develop character and integrity and with receptive adaptability there will be a great offering which will be happily received by many.

4 Being too aggressive with what you have to offer creates distrust and your abilities are wasted. Be more realistic and cease trying to impose yourself for the time being.

3 Your talents are too powerful to be used now. Keep a balanced attitude to yourself and keep from 'boiling over' with your offering. Then times will change for the better.

2 Your self-reliance is well established and those less balanced than yourself may try to overturn your position, but do not be bothered by them for your aim is good.

1 Though you are perhaps inexperienced and not in first place, your offering is appreciated and needed. Keep in mind the context as a whole even though you may be unbalanced.

51 AROUSING

THE IMAGE

Streaming Caves and Valleys Expand Spaciously into Lightning

The ears of the Dragon hear the rushing WATERS becoming the THUNDEROUS feet of the Dragon.

Repeated shocks bring tears or laughter. Mastering elementals is mastering dynamic movement at critical boundaries.

EARTHLY MOON CYCLE

Just after waxing half moon, excitement mounts and the release of energy in surprising actions can be beneficial. Binary 9.

JUDGMENT

AROUSING is the golden hexagram of the HUMBLE VIGIL-ANCE OF THE DRAGON changing into the APPROACH OF THE DRAGON. AROUSING is sometimes called shocking, associated with thunder, and is the innermost quality of the masculine principle permeating both the watery abdominal area and the whole nervous system. Your nervous system may receive a shock, but don't be unduly disturbed for this is natural at this time.

AROUSING is a time for the sudden release of stored energy which arouses movement and awakens. Awe and reverence are appropriate at this time. Be humble before the spontaneous power of the masculine principle in the cosmos. This is like springtime wherein the powerful rising forces stimulate extreme energy release. Remain calm in the midst of the jolting conditions and remain centered so that your energy is not scattered. Shock is beneficial when accompanied by insight. See what changes are needed and release the outworn.

MAN

For the man, AROUSING is the movement of the subtle current from the innermost core of his being. This is a time like spring where dormant incubative powers are suddenly brought into the light of day and new growth is rife. There may be unpredictable events and one must watch reactions and, with awareness of reactionary tendencies, strengthen character.

WOMAN

For a woman, AROUSING is a time of sudden inner vision. It is a good time to see spontaneous visions and dreams. It is not yet time to manifest such dreams and the visions may be terrifying. Whatever has laid dormant in the psyche will now become apparent and it is best to simply allow it to be revealed and to see clearly what needs to be changed.

The sudden flashes of insight at this time show a woman how her masculine principle may become effective. It is important to remain calm and have perspective and balance, especially during such times. Then activity which follows will be in accordance with the cosmic order.

LINES

-X- 6 Stop, for the extremity of shock would only cause you to behave unwisely and all beings around you would be afflicted. Your mind is not peaceful now. Retreat despite criticism from others.

-X- 5 Repeated shocks can be expected wherein communication is difficult. Remain as centered and calm as you can amidst the turmoil and all will be well.

-O- 4 The shock is so powerful you are stunned. Do nothing right now, for you were unprepared for this event which has cast you into confusion.

-X- 3 Arousing thunder upsets one's composure! This is a test of balance. You have some understanding of laws of change. This is a time to apply such laws.

-X- 2 Leaving your possessions in the face of shock is necessary, for there are sudden powers which force us to withdraw. What is temporarily lost will be refound in time.

-O- 1 Shock and fear can be stimulating to a needed change. Such unexpected ordeals are beneficial warnings.

52 KEEPING STILL

THE IMAGE

Reflecting Mountains Penetrate into Coals of Fire

The hands of the Dragon touch the MOUNTAINS through which the WATERS rush in streams, heard by ears of the Dragon.

No concentration, but just mindful with whole body and mind, being one with things. By being still one can encompass vast terrains. Effortless effort.

HEAVENLY MOON CYCLE

The heart of the azure Dragon in the depths of the night sky brings the point of absolute stillness. Binary 36.

JUDGMENT

KEEPING STILL reveals the CONTEMPLATION OF THE DRAGON transforming into the HUMBLE VIGILANCE OF THE DRAGON.

This is a time of stillness and inner composure whereby the masculine principle maintains contemplative discipline and also cosmic harmony with flowing reserves of energy. This might be compared with building dams and knowing when and where to lower them, whereby the valleys below become irrigated and nourished.

Now is a time to disengage from activities in the valleys or cities, however. It is well to go to the mountains or some quiet place, out of the usual routine of engagements you are involved with. As a consequence of a successful disengagement from worldly matters, you will better be able to nourish and be of assistance to people in need.

WOMAN

For a woman, KEEPING STILL is a change from a deliberate self-discipline in centering and meditation to creative activity. Remove yourself from relationships which are a drain on your energy and allow yourself to become quiet and receptive. This will open new channels of intuition and attunement to the cosmic order.

Do not try to do anything at first, but just realize a calm acceptance. When your thoughts cease and emotions settle into quietude, you may suddenly have a flash of insight never before known. This inspiration is the beginning of your potentially renewed power of creative action.

Above all, don't push or project into the future, but allow the present moment to come alive so that you know exactly what to do when. Actions will then be a creative meditation, restoring energy simultaneously with releasing it. This is a relaxed action in complete harmony with the cosmic order and a deeper springing forth of your true essence.

MAN

For a man, KEEPING STILL is a time of intuitive contemplation about matters of concern. Detach yourself from the object of your contemplation and try to see it just as it is. If you are able to reach a state of inner calm and serenity, even consciousness of your body will disappear.

Thinking is a definite deterrent now. Cease thinking and allow direct cognition to occur and your meditation will reach a deeper state of receptivity. True peace has intensity in the middle of it and the centering that needs to take place now will bring an inner knowing which will remove doubts and fears. This will lead to a return to your family, group or society with renewed reserves and a certainty which will nourish and strengthen everyone concerned.

LINES

6 Your composure has reached a mastery which stills spirit, mind and action. The true essence of things can be seen now for what they are.

5 Be still and listen through an open aware centering, then your thoughts will be clear and your words true.

4 Through a calm mind and body, true meditation is possible now. Distractions and laziness are now mastered and you can be at peace in centered awareness.

3 Cease trying to force things. Ambition is dangerous. Your restlessness is dangerous. Try to compose your mind and heart.

2 You should have kept still, but since you are now carried along by the flow of activity, there is nothing to do but let it run its course. This is unfortunate, but it will change.

1 Remain quiet and firm at the beginning of a new situation. Before moving, you need to know where you are moving to.

 53 DEVELOPMENT

THE IMAGE

Reflecting Jewels Penetrate into Coals of Fire

The hands of the Dragon reach for the space beyond the
MOUNTAINS *where the thighs of the Tiger move through the*
WIND.

The gradual growth of the oak tree never ceases and
overcomes the pithy swamp plants of quick ascension. Small
but penetrating insights build towards stability.

HEAVENLY MOON CYCLE

Meditation is now within and is present in all activities like a still fulcrum of knowning. The moon elixir is penetrating daily life. Binary 52.

JUDGMENT

DEVELOPMENT is the complete cycle of the transformation of the CONTEMPLATION OF THE DRAGON into the RETREAT OF THE TIGER.

This is a gradual and unceasing tendency of natural unfoldment. Step by step the complete cycle is known so that whatever affiliation you have now will last. Consistency in direction is important as you sort through possibilities and changes in life.

Traditional values, in so far as they reflect cosmic laws, can be trusted now as the best gradual way to develop. Do not make haste or impulsiveness a part of your life now. Move towards the union you desire with calm assurance, completing detail by detail all the things that need to be done.

Relationships tend to be positive now and it is beneficial to use this internal harmony for deepening bonds. By honest selfless love, there will be a step by step movement towards both stability and depth. By careful attention, gradualness can lead to trustworthiness. This includes a greater trust of yourself by your own constancy.

Engage in work for others with a sense of humility, revealing your talents only as they are needed. Friendships will endure by an unswerving firm direction and gentle consistent approach.

WOMAN

For a woman, DEVELOPMENT is a time of deep contemplation of all the changes of life and a movement slowly but surely to one's destiny. There is an inevitability to events now. Let it be. A strength is revealed in small consistent moves towards your highest and most complete aims. Ultimately this is the realization of the unity of all life.

MAN

For a man, DEVELOPMENT is a gradual permeating change whereby the realization of a vision of the whole cycle of life may be possible. It is appropriate now to do whatever is needed to perfect yourself towards the marriage of the masculine and feminine principles in yourself.

LINES

—o— 6 Climbing too high is not practical. Ideals must be seen in correspondence with what is really possible. When you see your relationship to a larger group there will be joy and harmony.

—o— 5 Even though there are difficulties and the harvest seems a long way off, the bond of love is strong and in the right time communication will be made.

—x— 4 Keep flexible and fluid for your resting place is only temporary. If you are uncomfortable move on to safer places.

—o— 3 Be careful about advancements now for this is a time to consolidate and not become aggressive. You can defend yourself but offend no one.

—x— 2 Communion, rest and happiness are yours to share with others now. Values of all kinds are to be shared.

—x— 1 You may feel insulted but don't be bothered by it, for patience is needed until criticism passes. Follow the law of nature and foundations are laid for later.

54 MARRYING MAIDEN

THE IMAGE

Streaming Caves and Valleys Explode into White Light

The mouth of the Tiger speaks in the LAKE reflecting the power of the feet of the Dragon running through THUNDER. Hasty marriages are temporary delights and long-term dangers. Lightning usually only strikes once in the same place.

EARTHLY MOON CYCLE

As the moon waxes, energies mount but may become imbalanced. The young and old mingle together only temporarily. Binary 11.

JUDGMENT

MARRYING MAIDEN shows the transformation of the POWER OF THE GREAT OF THE TIGER into the APPROACH OF THE DRAGON.

This is a very powerful situation, but not one in which to make advances. Now is a time when whatever you do or say is likely to be misunderstood because your energy is too aggressive and strong. This power is not in accord with the circumstances at hand.

The feminine and masculine principles are likely to be now strongly attracted, but not harmonious. Each sex may try to overcome the other. It is best not to try influencing anyone at this time.

There is very little harmony now for the feminine principle is too aggressive and dominating. The best one can do is witness the difficulty and try to cultivate gentleness where there is force and try to cultivate humility where there is arrogance.

MAN

For a man, MARRYING MAIDEN is a great change for it is a complete circuit of subtle energy. All aspects of a man may now be energized. Because of the overcharged energy, it is best not to say or to do anything. Rather it is best to try to subordinate yourself to the situation and seek understanding of what true values are yours.

It is unwise to give into the manipulations of the feminine principle or a woman near you, however. The more seductive this power to control may be the more dangerous it is. Maintain balance with all your deepest powers.

WOMAN

Receptivity is needed by a woman, but you may tend towards action and control over your partner or friend. This is a fruitless approach and the relationship will not last by these measures.

It is by vision that a woman can resolve this dangerous situation. She would do well to remain quiet, but vigilant and seeking of clarity of the whole situation. Long-range ideals can be developed now, based on an inner sense of values.

Remain true to your essential self and cease seeking control over others. Allow intuition to open, and take action on your highest sense of self-worth and clarity, according to the Tao.

LINES

—X— 6 The form is empty if true love is not present. Don't attempt to go through with a union founded on insincerity or compromises.

—X— 5 Put yourself in devoted service to others and there will be a harmonious marriage. Your virtue is the basis of this good fortune and best if continued in selfless devotion.

—O— 4 Hold off and develop yourself further before making a commitment to a relationship. Be true to your self and a more propitious relationship will unfold later.

—X— 3 Great suffering will result if you plunge ahead with this relationship for it compromises your true self.

—O— 2 Nothing great can be achieved with this relationship, but if you maintain the original vision, your devotion will bring harmony.

—O— 1 The relationship is lopsided, but can continue beneficially if you remain tactful and helpful. Though you have a partial view, sincerity will see you through.

55 ABUNDANCE

THE IMAGE

Rainbow Caves and Valleys Vaporize into Lightning

The ears of the Dragon hear the WATERS rushing into the LAKE reflected in the mouth of the Tiger.

Precise action brings forth fulfillments after long increases. Noon arrives only after morning has dawned.

EARTHLY MOON CYCLE

Three days before full moon is a time to envision the future beyond the immediate abundance of life. Sow seeds while giving out harvests. Binary 13.

JUDGMENT

In ABUNDANCE a zenith of the energy of the ESSENCE OF THE DRAGON is changing into the full expression of the POWER OF THE GREAT OF THE TIGER. This is a time of greatness and full expression of both nerve and circulatory energies. New directions can be tried and tendencies long in preparation may be accomplished and fulfilled. Now is a time of the HUMBLE VIGILANCE OF THE DRAGON rising like an essential perfume or elixir into the head where it emanates down through the whole body, giving you a radiance and glow. You don't need to think now so much as move on what you already intuitively know.

When the peak of fullness is reached, it is time to give out to others. Realize with confidence that what goes out creates space for renewed plenty. The warmth and clarity you may feel in the heart now will continue if you realize the infinite capacity of the wisdom of the heart and Tao.

MAN

For a man, ABUNDANCE reveals the subtle current in the brain as a great potential. As it descends to the base of the spine and rises up to the middle of the upper back and throat, you can feel it as a golden glow. This subtle current stimulates both heart and throat chakras. This is a time of great power and spontaneity. Do not hesitate to move with deep insights born now.

WOMAN

For a woman, the descent of the subtle currents transmutes any toxic conditions and purifies the whole body. As the subtle currents reach the base of the spine and rise up the back, over the crown of the head and down the front to the solar plexus center, there is a feeling of warmth and fulfillment.

This time is an awakening like high noon wherein what was before confused becomes clear, where what was before difficult becomes easy. Details take care of themselves.

LINES

—x— 6 Abundance has been yours but you have not fully appreciated it. Take nothing for granted. Your greatest possessions are integrity and friends, but now you are isolated out of pride.

—x— 5 People trust you now and help comes when it is needed. Be a receptive leader and the right people will bring good fortune.

—o— 4 Obstacles have been in your path but you can change adversity to advantage. By wise association and correct intention, beneficial results will come to all concerned.

—o— 3 You are getting in your own way by making so much of an issue. Calmly return to your center and realize your present disability.

—x— 2 There is some obscurity in the situation for you are trying too hard. Clarity is needed now more than will and effort. Others cannot trust you if you push ahead without illumination.

—o— 1 Go on to complete the project or relationship, for it is full and rich without going beyond measure. You work well together in clarity and action.

56 WANDERER

THE IMAGE

Rainbow Mountains Vaporize into Coals of Fire

The thighs of the Tiger move through the WIND as the Dragon listens to the vast WATERS.

The guest has complete freedom as long as he knows he is a guest. Release prosperity and new values emerge through journeys.

HEAVENLY MOON CYCLE

By shining the inner light of the waning moon elixir into the depths of being, the receptivity and humility appropriate to the traveler come into being. Binary 44.

JUDGMENT

In the WANDERER we see the transformation of the RETREAT OF THE TIGER into the HUMBLE VIGILANCE OF THE DRAGON.

This is a time to keep body and mind flexible and open to new situations. Keep reserved and retreat inwardly while remaining outwardly adaptive to situations as they arise. The circumstances in which you find yourself are not permanent. Everything is in a rapid state of change which can allow you to realize that your inmost self is not dependent on circumstances.

However, the changing conditions through which you pass are aids to breaking any rigid habits and unyielding attitudes. This will enable you to have greater perspective on the situation and to be a silent or friendly witness to the changes occurring now.

WOMAN

For a woman, the WANDERER is a dramatic time of change. It is well to make an effort to maintain an inner discipline on expressing too much. It is best to keep a quiet inner reserve while undergoing great changes and allow yourself space to contemplate new vantages. As the discipline takes over naturally, your state of intuitive receptivity will lead you spontaneously to the right places at the right time.

Then you will know who to approach when and will not hesitate to move in places and with persons you never before would imagine associating with. This open and flexible attitude will eventually give you great power to do any creative endeavor you wish.

If, along your journeys, something in a household needs to be fixed or changed, don't hesitate to be of service. By selflessly offering your newly-found abilities, you will become more and more certain of your true character and integrity amidst changing circumstances. Everything may seem temporary, but this is a true insight into life. The only constancy now is your humble witnessing of change.

MAN

For a man, the WANDERER is a time of clarification of the many vistas of life into a more holistic viewpoint. With this vision you can realize more clearly your place in the whole scheme. Being open to new experiences enables a contemplative attitude. Who you are can emerge more clearly out of the variegated happenings around you if you bring contemplation into pure receptivity. By being totally receptive your travels can bring you a great wealth of nourishment and inspiration.

This is not a time to find fault with others, but rather to pass over transgressions, making allowances or large space for others. Maintain inner integrity with reserve and a silent witnessing will change into a flow of exchange valuable to all concerned.

LINES

6 Being inconsiderate of others and minding other people's business, you have lost your own place. Your aims cannot be accomplished by going to such extremes.

5 You are successfully establishing yourself in new terrain or areas of expertise. Though it has been difficult, you have now hit the mark and are accepted in your new position.

4 Vigilance even while resting is necessary for there is uneasiness about a new situation. Protecting your accomplishments creates insecurity and restlessness.

3 Arrogance can destroy what you have. Cease interfering in matters that are not your affair. You may lose your lodgings as well as friends by stubbornness.

—x— 2 As a traveler you are benefitted by a good environment and your personal and financial resources are full. Because you are modest and reserved, people help you.

—x— 1 Don't be miserly or get involved in trivia when you are a guest. Be flexible and receptive to the customs where you are visiting or seeking entry.

57 PENETRATING

THE IMAGE

Reflecting Jewels Penetrate into Comets and Stars

The eyes of the Tiger envision the FIRE speeded by the WIND, enveloping the thighs of the Tiger.

Repetition of practice creates stimulation. Invisible as the wind the persistent power of growing trees conquers great rocks and stones. Continue efforts.

HEAVENLY MOON CYCLE

When wind is repeated the movement forward is intense being. The moon elixir now pervades your whole atmosphere. Binary 54.

JUDGMENT

PENETRATING is the INNER TRUTH OF THE TIGER changing into the RETREAT OF THE TIGER.

Essences and hidden qualities are now at their apogee. The invisible is penetrating into the visible, but cannot yet be seen. Gradual and subtle transition is essential now. Gentleness and adaptability are needed so that clarity can shine through. Anonymity and inconspicuousness are essential now. Do not make a show or try to force your way into anything. Your goals will be revealed through long-term gentle penetration in humble purposes. Patience and slow movement in a single direction will eventually have success.

You have a good heart and can trust it. So allow yourself to bend with the wind. Only a stupid person stands up in a cyclone! Allow subtle energy to accumulate and it will sustain you through all trials. Allow yourself to be as pervasive as the wind and giving no resistance to change, you will find growth all around and within you.

WOMAN

For a woman, PENETRATING is a time wherein it is important to realize that the invisible and often unconscious forces are the most all-pervading. It is a time to feel out all aspects of the situation and take action only when all is in accord with the clarity of the heart. The goal is all-important and by slow penetration to the source of gentleness as love, you will fulfill it.

MAN

For a man, PENETRATING is a long and gentle change of allowing the love of the heart to pervade one's being until clarity comes. Enduring and consistent effort can be made to direct thoughts, feelings and actions towards a single large aim.

Concentration is good at this time and should be used to gradually realize your goals.

LINES

—O— 6 By subservient strategies and schemes to influence others you will lose integrity. Inferior people only are attracted.

—O— 5 Keep a clear head and gentle heart in the present situation for there are dangerous influences near. Alert evaluation is worthy if you manage to keep constant. The reform benefits all.

—X— 4 Once you are past your temptations and take positive action, there will be many resources and you can successfully make offerings.

—O— 3 Humiliation comes from being overly submissive when you lose confidence. There are delusions which lead to loss of faith. Find out what is true.

—O— 2 Discriminate between fantasy and reality and eliminate foolish delusions and you will have success. Sound decisions are called for and swift actions.

—X— 1 Hesitation creates a drifting undisciplined way of life. Like a warrior you need firm intentions now.

58 JOYOUS

THE IMAGE

Streaming Sands Explode into White Light

The mouth of the Tiger reveals LAKES reflected in the FLAMING eyes of the Tiger.

Joy is multiplied by being reflected in the mirror of the eyes of others. Joy in work with people of common values nullifies toil.

EARTHLY MOON CYCLE

With the waning moon, the inner joy is doubly increased by the silent reverberation of serene minds. Binary 27.

JUDGMENT

The POWER OF THE GREAT OF THE TIGER changes in the JOYOUS to the INNER TRUTH OF THE TIGER. This is a time to allow one's expressive power to turn from self-expression into that of joyous, optimistic encouragement of others.

The INNER TRUTH of the matter is that one is not separate from others and this realization in practical life means being able to joyfully make sacrifices for others . . . knowing the inseparable aspect of spiritual union. Kindness and generosity are the fountainhead of the JOYOUS.

This is a time of deep communication and openness to the needs of others. One can test ideals on whether they work with others. The true test is in relationship.

MAN

For a man, the JOYOUS is the current of subtle energy rising up the back of the head and descending as deep inner CONTEMPLATION before it rises into the cauldron of the heart where INNER TRUTH is found. The POWER OF THE GREAT OF THE TIGER 'in the blood' is to understand others and assist them in realizing the direct truth in the heart of hearts.

This awareness naturally brings people into accord. For a man, the time of the JOYOUS is a time to realize his feminine power by detaching from fruits of actions and allowing the force of INNER TRUTH to work naturally.

WOMAN

For a woman, the JOYOUS is a time wherein her power of creative manifestation is to be brought to bear joyful fruits through accordance with INNER TRUTH. The subtle current moves from her great reservoir of energy in the solar plexus down through the sex center where the co-creation of arts, services, culture is born through her.

In your heart of hearts all that you have brought forth is to be purified and bathed in the 'blood' of the pure spirit of the Tao.

Detachment from the fruits of one's labors is essential now, or else all that is created will be polluted by attachment and ego. This is an opportunity to rid oneself (and all those around) of anything rigid, dogmatic and purely habitual by the force of INNER TRUTH.

LINES

—x— 6 By leaning out to please others you have lost your sense of values and are vulnerable to external forces which can lead to great suffering. Joy is found within. Look there for it.

—o— 5 Watch yourself for you are tempted to be drawn into a scheme which exploits others. This can only lead to negative results and unhappiness. Discriminate and remain alert.

—o— 4 Choose between superior and inferior joys, for in the present situation it is impossible to have both. Curb your lower desires and great happiness will be yours.

—x— 3 Flattery to those above you displays weakness which will only temporarily give you joy. Humiliation results from such transient and shifting words and deeds.

—o— 2 Being constant to true friends and maintaining integrity gives you true joy. The trust that is established now strengthens all concerned.

—o— 1 True joy is within and comes from an independence which is true and spontaneous. Mutual harmony results from being true to cosmic law.

59 DISSOLVING

THE IMAGE

6 Vast Seas of Jewels Condense into Comets and Stars

The eye of the Tiger sees the FLAMING beauty of fires evaporating WATERS into the hands of the CONTEMPLATING Dragon.

As water dissolves salt, loving kindness is a solvent for the hardest, most rigid patterns. Proportion sets right boundaries and dispersion dissolves wrong boundaries.

HEAVENLY MOON CYCLE

Just after dark moon is a time when the unconscious powers are drawn up and past wrongs forgiven. There is no possibility of being who you were before. Accept the new inner radiance. Binary 50.

JUDGMENT

DISSOLVING is the INNER TRUTH OF THE TIGER changing into the CONTEMPLATION OF THE DRAGON.

The break-up of old patterns, blockages and rigid beliefs is now given an opportunity. This is a time to release personal clinging and discover universal values which can bring you into greater accord with others. Realize that there is a cosmic order and plan so that you can harmonize with it.

Sacrifice any tendencies which oppose the cosmic order and you will find a renewal of energy through truth. Do not isolate yourself now, but unite with others in gentleness. Mutuality comes through an awakening to common values which benefit all of mankind. Dissolving of selfish interests will bring a sense of transcendence which might even beneficially express itself as a celebration or ritual of renewal.

WOMAN

For a woman, DISSOLVING is a time of great insight. Old anxieties and fears can be dissolved through quiet meditations. Don't attempt to control anything outwardly, but bring a devoted heart into knowing only reality. Once insight is found, there will be enthusiasm to share with others your sense of well-being. Others' response to your insights may become a danger of exclusiveness. Avoid all tendencies to create cults, sects or factions.

The kindness of the heart is to be spread to all of humanity. Exclude no one in your heart of hearts and contemplate ways of bringing about harmony in specific groups.

MAN

For a man, DISSOLVING is a time wherein the insights of the heart overflow into a warmth and gentleness which can be used in great service to others. Bring the intuitions of the heart up into great inspirations which you can communicate to others. This can lead to a vision and commitment to a project or event which will bring significant contributions to your society. Devote yourself to nurturing this vision by contemplation and the energy-field of loving gentleness will circulate to dissolve separatism among your associates.

LINES

6 Move away from the situation if you must, for there is a crisis at hand. This is not avoidance in this case, but the best expression of concern for others as well as yourself.

5 There are wild influences present but you can have a taming influence if you remain constant in gentle persuasion. Like a great sweat or fever, it is best to break through the present situation with true inspiration and gifts. Then others will follow.

4 By expressing values which transcend personal issues, people who were formerly in conflict come into accord. By dedicating yourself to others, you are helped.

3 There is no regret in putting aside personal wishes for the welfare of the whole of humanity. Dissolve all egotism and common aims will be clear whereby many will pledge themselves.

2 Rescuing others who are in even greater need than yourself will be beneficial at this time. Don't hesitate to help and you will also be helped.

1 Conflict is present but seeing it early enables you to disperse discord, whereby cooperation among friends supports the whole community.

60　　PROPORTION

THE IMAGE

Vast Seas of Sands Condense into White Light

The feet of the Dragon run on THUNDER where FLAMES are consumed in the eyes of the Tiger.

Days set the frame for a week and seasons set the limits of a year. Knowing the right measure is maintaining harmonious order.

EARTHLY MOON CYCLE

The waning moon sets limits on energy so that inner awakening increases. Right appropriation of moving and ceasing clarifies boundaries. Binary 19.

JUDGMENT

PROPORTION is the APPROACH OF THE DRAGON changing into the INNER TRUTH OF THE TIGER. The arousing power of the Dragon in the nervous system must be restrained, not by force, but by INNER TRUTH.

The force of the masculine principle is to be evoked, but not expressed by aggression. Rather, the limits of force are found through the INNER TRUTH of the feminine principle in the heart.

Extravagance and self-indulgence of all kinds — whether of money, emotions, thoughts, ideals, energy — must all be curbed by the realization of inner cosmic law. Here awareness is needed to balance the arousing, advancing quality of the Dragon so that motion will be regulated in an orderly way, according to the INNER TRUTH.

MAN

For a man, this means a great change, from the arousal of increasing yang energy at the base of the spine, up the back and down the front, to become CONTEMPLATION and finally refined in the cauldron of the heart. Self-expression needs to be refined to universal principles so that the purity of the heart shines out in the art or activity participated in.

Extremes of all kinds are not so much to be avoided as transmuted into the middle path of moderation by awareness.

WOMAN

For a woman, PROPORTION is not as great a transformation as for a man. Yet it is equally significant. For the shocking arousal of the APPROACH OF THE DRAGON is in dreams and visions. Such dreams and visions must be brought down to earth in your power of manifestation, according to the INNER TRUTH of the natural law.

Visions should not be indulged in, but made clear, shorn of all attachments and brought into the realm of manifest realization. Neither radical reform nor weak contemplation are appropriate. Rather, you can now express yourself by being accommodating to the truth of the situation. It is a time of purifying visions and ideals according to the common good and cosmic order.

The feminine highest intuition of the heart is needed to curb aroused fantasies and turn them into clear visions and creative imagination.

LINES

—x— 6 Stop being so restrictive. This is not showing your sense of proportion, for you are expecting too severe a discipline. Become more flexible and accepting and the high standards you have will more easily be reached.

—o— 5 When you are able to accomplish much through restricted resources, this is a good sign. You have regulated your life in habitual good measure and others respect you for it.

—x— 4 Rhythm is the basis of good proportion. Don't argue over rigid principles but follow a rhythmically viable plan which can bring about powerful results.

—x— 3 You are beginning to recognize your lack of proportion in the matter. You are rightfully seeing that extravagance is wasteful.

—o— 2 If you keep holding back reserves, the mounting energy will be too much for you. Distribute according to need when the time arises, for it is dangerous to accumulate beyond measure.

—o— 1 Quietly gather your energies in a safe place at this time for you don't yet have abundance. Restrict your areas of influence and remain calm amidst difficulties.

 **61 INNER TRUTH**

THE IMAGE

Vast Seas of Jewels Condense into White Light

The eyes of the Tiger circle in FLAMES around the heart of all matter.

The fires of the heart burn away all impurities when the trials of life awaken the sleeping woman. Being true to itself, the Tiger leaps.

HEAVENLY MOON CYCLE

Self-reflecting, intense inner awakening does not revolve as part of the moon cycle, but is a pivot point of centering through truth. The aura radiates from a still center. Binary 51.

JUDGMENT

INNER TRUTH is the heart and essence of the Tiger. There is no change here. It is what it is and whoever sees how it is does not question further. Now is a time when all barriers, masks, prejudices, likes and dislikes fall away in the face of the realization of the truth. Through the clarity of this insight and knowledge of the heart of the matter, no argument or discussion is necessary.

Now a penetrating insight reveals itself and is self-evident to everyone concerned. Clarity and openness of heart will reveal the inner essence of your true nature, and this surrender to pure being will enable you to see others clearly. Give up everything now except the truth and trust the Tao.

MAN AND WOMAN

INNER TRUTH is the natural accord with cosmic harmony through the deep feminine principle in the heart of hearts for both men and women.

At this time, one can give others a vision of the truth without losing perspective or one's own interests. It becomes clear that one's true self-interests are in accordance with the common good, which is in harmony with cosmic law.

If you need to speak or act, allow the INNER TRUTH to speak through your heart and people will give loyalty without effort. It may be a time of living quietly with a true vision of the common values of humanity.

LINES

—o— 6 You are reaching too high just now and losing your balance. Past successes do not assure repetitive results; for if you are too ambitious even about inner realization you delude yourself and others.

—o— 5 Inner truth and ability to communicate it brings about a state of great good fortune. People gather around deep sincerity and integrity and will be benefitted by your example at this time.

—x— 4 It is time to discriminate between greater and lesser truths. If you choose the greater truth you may leave some people behind but your realization of the cosmic order will be much greater.

—x— 3 By relying too much on others you may come to either great joy or great sorrow. Only you yourself know if it is worth extending yourself in this way, for you may lose your center of truth.

—o— 2 Firm leadership is present because of inner truth which is proclaimed to the whole community. Sharing true insight brings many people into accord whereby a resonance of hearts creates a strong bond.

—o— 1 Remain single-pointed and steadfast in inner truth; otherwise confusion will come from conflicting aims. Peace has a strong center in truth.

62 HUMBLE VIGILANCE

THE IMAGE

Rainbow Caves and Valleys Vaporize into Coals of Fire

The ears of the Dragon listen to the sounds of the rippling WATERS of cosmic vibrations.

Flowing with the Tao is like the old man who dove into cascades and came up with the whirl. The light floats and the heavy sinks.

EARTHLY MOON CYCLE

A point of stillness outside the moon cycles, this is a time of inner transition wherein doing nothing and witnessing all is supreme. Binary 12.

JUDGMENT

HUMBLE VIGILANCE is the immutable golden hexagram wherein the HUMBLE DRAGON is attentive to the right measure of all things in view.

It is important now to remain balanced and avoid all extremes, including undertaking new or large tasks. It is task enough just now to tide through the present transition with clarity and humility. Refine your energy and insights and the forces which seemingly seek to overpower you will diminish their force. Regeneration comes from within when virtue is able to withstand temptations of excess and retaliation.

MAN AND WOMAN

For both men and women, now is a time to remain in an openly modest position and to listen to the flowing currents of change in life all around you. You may have gut instincts on what is right and it is well to trust them at this time, but not take vigorous action. Rather, allow changes to happen by regular and consistent duty rather than by sweeping measures. Gentle penetration is better now than opposing arguments. If you have an opponent and he or she is overbearing, it is well to let their energy to spend itself before you make even a humble suggestion.

Rather than expending a lot of thought and energy or money on the situation, it is best now to relax and work only on small details. Keep a low profile in everything you do now and obstructions will clear in time if you just maintain your daily chores. Do not ignore things happening around you, but also do not react to them. This entails a state of humble vigilance which will recharge your battery and bring in reserves which right now you do not have. All is well just as it is.

LINES

—x— 6 You have lost your humble vigilance in attempts to reach too high. Lofty claims and ideals will not substitute for reality. Drop your ambitions and aggressiveness in spiritual matters and return to ordinary daily life.

—x— 5 You have great energy, but are not yet competent to meet the demand. Stay humble and seek assistance from others of talent and yours also will be brought out in the right time.

—O— 4 Don't be restless and forge ahead now for slow inward perseverance is what is needed. Keep humbly alert or you will meet resistance.

—O— 3 You are exposing yourself to dangers because of pride and exaggerated force. Be careful for you are susceptible to flattery due to lack of humility.

—x— 2 Remain low and help others near you. It is not time for you to shine in the limelight for there is simple everyday work to be done without making an issue of it.

—x— 1 Simplicity and ordinary concerns on everyday life are to be tended now. If you try to exceed normal limits you will draw disaster upon yourself.

63   AFTER COMPLETION

THE IMAGE

Reflecting Sands Penetrate into Lightning

The bellies of the Tiger and Dragon throughout the EARTH circle into the pure white light of HEAVEN.

When sap is drawn up the stem of great trees, the danger of fire draws near. Water above fire cannot endure except as cycle. The complete ring is golden.

EARTHLY MOON CYCLE

Moving towards waning half moon, it is time to anticipate the future wherein new preparations need be made beyond what has been accomplished. Binary 21.

JUDGMENT

AFTER COMPLETION is the UNION OF THE TIGER AND DRAGON, wherein the RECEPTIVE or negative principle becomes the CREATIVE or positive principle. This is a complete polarization wherein an exchange is so complete as to be a fusion. This is not just balance or posed equilibrium, but an actual union. Such a union is irrevocable and recorded for all time and leaves both the masculine and feminine aspects open to totally new changes.

This is like the void after a generous release of energy. This void is to be experienced as a relief from all self-images, desires, delusions, fears or notions about who you are or what to do.

Make use of this time by realizing the inherent union of opposites and experience it deeply so that when you are living in opposition again, this unity will enable you to remain peaceful. Fire and water are opposite elements which are now integrated within you like an alchemical garden of satisfaction. This is no time to become forgetful and overly confident just because momentarily the tension is relaxed, however. Completion of one thing is the beginning of another. Look deeply into what you have just completed to find the seeds of new birth.

MAN

For a man, AFTER COMPLETION is the change of the RECEPTIVE principle in the sexual center up into the central unconscious channel of his being wherein heart and mind are linked. Then comes an arousal to activity and great power which culminates as positive CREATIVE ideas. Vigilance and attention are important aspects of this transformation so that whatever is culminated is not lost as mere energy or matter; but instead is brought from awareness into love and wisdom in heart and mind, as the gem of truth in the 'Jade Gate'.

WOMAN

For a woman, your intuition, like a flash out of the blue, turns into vision and then polarizes as fruitful CREATIVE manifestation . . . in family, social order, the arts of daily life. Since, in AFTER COMPLETION, a woman starts with intuition, all else is part of the creative conscious process of manifesting in daily life through outward actions. The fusion of the male and female within you manifests as a climax of your waking life activity.

LINES

—x— 6 At the end of the project you have fallen to the great danger of making false assumptions that your accomplishments will last. Over-confidence after completing a great task is exceedingly dangerous.

—o— 5 A big show of your successes is less meaningful than a small sincere action in daily life. Don't be wasteful and ruin, by extravagance, what you have achieved.

—x— 4 Keep vigilant of the possibility that your completions are not constant. Consider others.

—o— 3 You have entered a great task and have the capacity to complete it but you will need qualified helpers. Keep open to possibilities, work hard and success will be yours despite temporary tiredness.

—x— 2 Temporary delays in completing the task at hand need not cause worry, for they will pass of their own accord. Cease trying to intervene.

—o— 1 Be careful when you set out upon a great task and reflect on all the issues before taking action. Pressures mount naturally and if you are careful and considerate, the right sequence of unfoldment will be found.

64   BEFORE COMPLETION

THE IMAGE

Streaming Mountains Explode into Comets and Stars

The head of the white light of HEAVEN changes the Tiger and Dragon into the belly of the dark EARTH.

Everything in heaven and earth regenerates by its own methods. But that with life regenerates better than stones and that with spirit regenerates above all. Prepare for the end which brings new beginnings.

HEAVENLY MOON CYCLE

The moon elixir increases in the heavenly cycle with the decrease of moonlight. Consciousness is above the unconscious and when a reversal takes place, it is time to begin. Binary 42.

JUDGMENT

BEFORE COMPLETION is the CREATIVE changing into the RECEPTIVE wherein the UNION OF THE TIGER AND DRAGON is moving towards fulfillment.

This is a time of great transformation. Chaos can now be changed into order. The dynamic character of your present situation can take a new pattern of possibilities which can endure. It will not happen by itself, however.

Different aspects of the situation are pulling in multitudes of directions and it is timely that you apply voice and effort to make clear a unifying goal. Evaluate all aspects of the problem and make arrangements to bring them into complementary concordance. Polarities are at their optimum and this prepares the way for a great transformation of creative powers into stability.

WOMAN

For a woman, BEFORE COMPLETION is a time when creative manifestation has come to an end and it is time to apply effort to evaluate what has been accomplished. This insight in itself brings a completion through an intuitive communion. To do this is not to sit back and do nothing, but to apply discipline to methods of meditation or paths of insight which enable you to listen to others' views in relation to a common goal.

Do not be impatient, for the interests which you have creatively involved yourself in are now about to yield a harvest. This will come only when you have completely released yourself from all attachments to what you have done.

MAN

For a man, BEFORE COMPLETION is a time when creative inspirations are in abundance. Allowing this abundance to become effective depends on your ability to see clearly into the situation, evaluate it and allow the various aspects to come together by their intrinsic qualities. This takes a contemplative and receptive ability on your part after first communicating your profusion of inspiration.

There is a danger of continuing your creative expression either too long or too short. If you express too much, those around you will be lost as to what their role is in the whole scheme. If you express too little and expect things to happen without your awareness, there will be nothing to evaluate. To resolve something is to realize the right measure of giving and receiving to all.

LINES

—o— 6 Don't get so excited by your achievement that you lose control of yourself. People cannot trust someone who is in excessive raptures.

—x— 5 Humility and enlightenment together create great confidence and can bring in qualities of a new culture based on the cosmic order. You now have inner light and the power to overcome many current difficulties.

—o— 4 Maintain uprightness and through hardship and work the goal can be achieved. Continue to the end in courage and discipline, without grasping for rewards.

—x— 3 With the right helpers the task can be completed but there is a great present danger. You can move out of the danger with clear perseverance towards your highest aim.

—o— 2 Cease restlessness. This is no time for action. Make cautious preparations and keep singleness of vision and the right time will come.

—x— 1 Inexperienced in the matter at hand, you will come to disgrace if you plunge ahead without evaluating your abilities, resources and the immensity of the task.

PART III

Commentaries on I Ching
and the
Golden Hexagrams

Commentary 1
Polarities and wholeness:
basic structure of the I Ching

The *I Ching* is a book that reveals how to conduct life with wisdom. It is a meditative book and practical book. The Golden Tiger and Dragon Oracle gives guidance on a new method of using the *I Ching* based on Taoist yoga, symbolized by the union of the Tiger and the Dragon, or feminine and masculine principles (see Commentaries 6–8). The passage to this union is in consciousness.

The roots of disease as well as health are in consciousness. Even before the scientific revolution of the nineteenth century, the Renaissance revealed signs of the separation of body and mind as well as the repression or shadowing of the spirit. The present day predicament, in health, education and economics, can be traced to patterns of consciousness seeded hundreds of years prior to now. Once the momentum of events has reached a certain stage of bifurcation, it is as irreversible as the branching of a tree into smaller and smaller segments.

The trend of continuity is in the direction of greater and greater separation: of specialized fields of study, of rich and poor, of body and mind, of science and spiritual practices; but there is a pattern which offers hope. Like the bud on the end of a forked stem, a whole new process unfolds, holding the promise of forthcoming fruit and seed.

If one had never observed the budding process and saw the ever branching of stems, one would find it unpredictable that a bud would emerge at a certain end of the branching process. It IS predictable if one knows the whole process of a tree.

In order to realize the whole of any phenomenon, it is necessary that the absolute poles or complementary extremes be known. Otherwise all characteristics are only arbitrary and incomplete lists. Evidence shows that this world works on the basis of polarity and that it is regenerative in its 'fruit' or harvest phase.

Our relativistic culture has been hypnotized by Einstein's Theory of Relativity by generalizing that 'all things are relative.'

To realize wholeness we have to get beyond relativities into crystal clear awareness of what the source of polarity really means and *live it*. The *I Ching* is a book of wholeness. Its use is practical and spiritual at once.

If we ask what is the greatest wholeness we can imagine or know, then we must go beyond light and dark or even the whole electromagnetic spectrum and acknowledge what the ancient Chinese called the T'ai Chi. In its original meaning, T'ai Chi means ridgepole.

The still more primal beginning, called Wu Chi, was represented by the circle or the *Unity* of this primal polarity. Unity represented by the circle is very important for it indicates that what the ancient Chinese called the yin and yang are a primary polarity and not secondary or tertiary (see Commentary 3). They are not relative dualities but primary polarities.

Wu Chi is absolute quiescence, involving no polarity. We can represent it by a pure white space:

T'ai Chi is the yin and yang polarity of opposites emerging out of Wu Chi:

The further sub-division of yin and yang yields a four-fold pattern:

These four are called the Four Emblematic Figures and are generally given the assignments:

	Greater yang
	Smaller yin
	Smaller yang
	Greater yin

In the Tiger and Dragon Oracle, we use the Four Emblematic

figures in such a way as to see parallels of the sixty-four hexagrams with the more fundamental eight trigrams (see Appendix 1).

The final sub-division of yin and yang yields the eight trigrams which fall naturally in the order of the Fu Hsi or pre-Heaven diagram:

The whole unfoldment from the one to the ten thousand things is through the eight trigrams which, combined, create the hexagrams creating the total possibilities of sixty-four:

The sons are the principles of motion in three stages:

THUNDER eldest son: arousing, instigating of movement
WATER   middle son: sinking, abysmal, danger or critical
        stage of motion
MOUNTAIN   youngest son: rest, stillness or completion of
        motion

The daughters are the principles of devotion or emotion

WIND   eldest daughter: gently penetrating
FIRE   middle daughter: clarity, clinging, brightness, beauty
LAKE   youngest daughter: serenity, fulfillment.

The sixty-four hexagrams are constructed out of the combinations of the qualities of the eight trigrams.

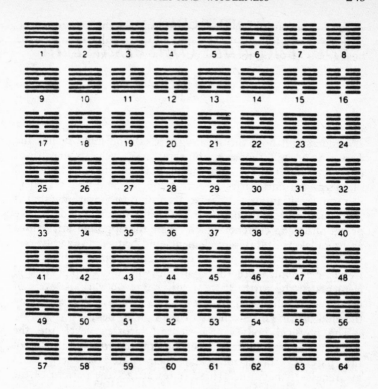

The Sixty-Four Hexagrams

Commentary 2
The Tao and Universal Laws of Harmony

To understand how the *I Ching* works, one must realize the Taoist awareness that everything in the universe is in various degrees of vibrational energy. Subtle and gross, the manifestation of energy currents varies in both frequency and quality. There is a universal law of resonance, according to vibrations, that is both qualitative and quantitative. It is the negative and positive or yin and yang currents which create the apparent attractions and repulsions of different elements and beings in the universe.

The human being is a unity, embodying innumerable frequencies which are found in the sun, moon, planets and elements of the earth. Patterns of energy on various levels of subtlety are influenced by the various 'bodies' represented by the chakras or subtle centers of the human being.

The physical body is the densest, grossest level and the quality of its manifestation depends on the time and place of the parents' conception, and their state of energy and awareness at that time. These states attract the pattern of the particular individual conceived.

The more subtle 'bodies' of emotional, mental, spiritual, intuitive, etc., are influenced by the conditions of awareness of the parents as well as factors of the position of the stellar and planetary bodies. All this may seem strange to those conditioned to believe that patterns and 'objects' in the universe are separate entities.

The Ch'i or subtle life-energy is the base or medium of all vibrations. It is without tangibility and yet it is the all-pervading 'life-breath' in which all tangible entities have their being.

The source of Ch'i is Tao, for in the Taoist view, the Tao is the source and eternal reality of both the manifest and unmanifest realms. Tao exists 'before' and 'after' the universe is born or passes away . . . for Tao is timeless and changeless and yet is totally fluid, spontaneous and whole.

There is room for everything in the Tao. The myriads of

'things' go back to the source, the mystery of mysteries which is Tao. It is serene in the center and the center is everywhere. There is no opinion or prejudice which does not fall away at the source. The power of the Tao is powerless and yet all fears and desires are completely washed away by it. He who is one with the Tao dies many times before death and thus becomes indestructible. Though the body may wither and decay, the spirit does not suffer and is beyond all danger.

Thus union with the Tao is not of one entity with another, but is the revelation of that which is eternally one. Non-being and being are here not separate.

Out of the stillness which is the Tao rises all movement. When in meditation, awareness of the material world ceases, there are visions. When visions cease, there is light. When light ceases, there is darkness and nothing . . . the non-being and being in unity of the unborn. The unborn never dies. The Tao is unborn.

Through the Tao and the awareness of it through the *I Ching*, we can learn to cease doing (with ego). Then the purity of being is revealed and all things are done naturally. When one is finished with the outer lights, the inner lights shine. In general, in the past, the Orientals have been more active in finding quiescence. The Western world either waits for quiescence or never bothers with it. Now the Oriental and Western tendencies are reversing and this ancient oracle can give Westerners peace of mind.

The spirit of the Tao is in everything. It is through the 'emptiness' or 'hole' of the vortexes of yin and yang that it manifests. The qualitative essences emanate from the 'holes', which creates 'wholes' from the One through the Many. These patterns of the vortexes of yin and yang are the frequencies of subtle energy or Ch'i.

Commentary 3
Yin and Yang Energy Patterns and Change

Yin and yang are like the filling and emptying of vessels. The yang lines are like fullness itself, radiating light. The yin lines are like the emptiness of space wherein energy flows in and out. The vessels of life are 'made' of yin and yang, emptiness and fullness, ever changing. All the hexagrams derive from yin and yang. Unceasing motion, the patterns of change nevertheless have temporary states which we call the hexagrams.

In the same way, every person and creature is in a state of flux . . . the body, feelings, thoughts, intuition are continuously changing, not only in content, but in form. The vessel itself is changed. In this sense, the hexagrams can be seen as vessels of emptiness and fullness, like positive and negative. (There is no *value judgment* of positive and negative any more than of the dual charges of electricity or the crests and troughs of a wave!) Form and content are not separate in the hexagrams.

All form has limits. Limits may seem 'bad' or 'good' to a person experiencing them, but like all value judgments, these are *reactions* to the states of change. The states of change themselves are neutral. We may feel that birth is good and death is bad, but both birth and death are like gates through the circle of life, which is continuous. It is the *attachment* to specific states of change that brings suffering. Therefore no hexagram is bad or good in itself. Each is appropriate to the situation.

Life continues through changes and is not a preservation or mummifying process. Civilizations may crumble because of an attempt to rigidify, but life goes on. When something dies, it is simply returning the vessel of exchange to the ground of its being. The elements return to the elements and the life-spirit returns to the 'after-death' state appropriate to it. *The changes go on until there is complete freedom from attachment to one or another changing condition.*

This freedom may be more possible if we can realize the specific change in relation to the whole. That is why this book

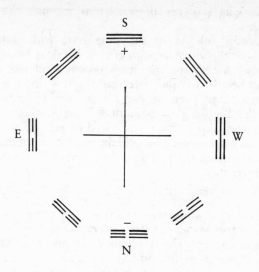

1 Pre-heaven

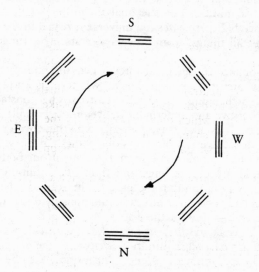

2 Later-heaven

is emphasizing patterns of wholeness through the Golden Hexagrams.

We identify fullness or the yang state with source; and emptiness or the yin state with effects. It might be argued the other way around, for emptiness becomes fullness and vice versa; but because of time's irreversible arrow, there is a reason for source being yang in our visible world. Time is yang because the 'Big Bang' of radiational (yang) nuclear and stellar events creates time in the eternal void of yin. All the changes are like yang spermatic codes filling the vacuity of yin; and in turn yin emptying itself of yang like birth of time out of the womb of eternity.

The hexagrams are changing states, in consciousness and in outer conditions. There is no stasis any more than there is in water. Even in a windless, currentless lake, there is motion of molecules. The hexagrams are, rather, *temporary patterns of qualitative energy*. The molecules, atoms and sub-atomic particles in water are magnitudes of change.

The hexagrams signify innumerable magnitudes of change in sixty-four qualities. What makes them qualitative and not merely quantitative is the evaluative function of the whole mind. This mind is not the analytic rational mind, but the intelligence that permeates the universe revealed in the intricate designs of all things, from flowers to stars. The Taoists call it Tao.

By resonance to this great intelligence, the human spirit can 'know' whatever it needs to know. Whatever is known at any one time is changing into another pattern. This constant dance is non-repetitive and impermanent, even though similar patterns may recur. It is like wave-patterns with new water running through them. Every seven years our bodies have new cells and every day new atoms come in and go out of our bodies. Even more rapid are our feelings and thoughts. Intuition is faster still. It is by intuition that the pure qualities of the changes can be apprehended best, for intuition functions by direct resonance with the energy flow of the Tao.

The Tao is always present tense. Reason as well as the senses are relatively past tense. Intuition is closer to the present. Like a vast landscape of inner and outer dimensions, each hexagram is a temporary view changing into another temporary view. Some conditions, like rocks, change relatively more slowly than the water and the clouds, but all is changing. The hexagrams are like snapshots of a 360 degree landscape which is also an interior panorama of the human body, not only on the physical level but including energy fields.

The energy fields within the great whole of continuously enduring change is the 'uncarved block' of the Taoists. Direct awareness of the changeless through all changes is Tao which has no beginning or ending. The Tao is life, which is eternal. Only beings with beginnings and endings, births and deaths, change.

Nowhere is there complete repetition of changes. Even if the same hexagram with the same changing lines recurs for the same person's oracle, the person's state of consciousness is different and will interpret the hexagram differently. Each time the spiral of patterns comes around, you become either more aware, more pure and clear, or the opposite.

Awareness of the currents of life-energy flowing all around, within and without us, enables us to open up to and flow with the great energy currents, vortexes and eddies. This direct awareness enables what we need to flow to us at the right time and right place in resonance with the Tao.

The Tao is an infinitely subtle web of vortexes and waves. The eight trigrams can be understood as phases of a turning wave or the complete water-cycle from the source, through lakes and the mist evaporating from surface waters into clouds, through the wind and rain forming into waterfalls and rivers down into underground streams into the sea. Such is the play of yin and yang.

Commentary 4
Qualities of the eight trigrams in correlation to the landscape, parts of the body and wave patterns

Since the inner and outer 'worlds' are one, when we deeply experience a landscape, we also deeply experience ourselves. We might compare the qualities of the eight trigrams to the water-cycle in a landscape as well as to parts of the body which are symbolic of certain states of consciousness.

The fountainhead or WATER SOURCE corresponds to Ch'ien ☰, the creative HEAVEN. The Chinese attribute this trigram to the head of the human body. The head is one source. A deeper source might be seen as the solar plexus or the belly, which the Chinese ascribe to the trigram of K'un, the receptive EARTH. This is the opposite pole of the source which corresponds to the sea as compared to the sources of water in the heavens.

Tui ☱, the joyous LAKE, can clearly be seen in the high mountain lakes in the landscape which give us great joy and purity. Lakes are bursting with life as are all things in their budding stage where the creativity of Ch'ien has entered into them and a sense of freedom is immanent. The Tui trigram corresponds to the mouth in the Chinese system, that which receives nourishment and also gives out speech. The first 'vibrations' are really formed in Tui for this is the 'Word in the beginning of Creation' (to make a Biblical analogy).

The creative source as Ch'ien is really invisible to us just as our own heads are (since our eyes are inside of our heads)! The mirrors we look into to be assured that we have heads are more like the LAKE of Tui. The true source of the creative HEAVEN is like blinding light. The first vibrations are experienced in Tui, both as chemical activity in our food, molecular activity in our

252

breathing and sound activity combined with breath in speech and song.

Only 'after' this pure vibration is the sap of life formed out of a kind of distillation of vibrations from the LAKE of Tui. This is the clarity and intelligence and clinging quality of Li, the FIRE. In the landscape, it is the solar principle, and in the water cycle, it is like the rising mist from the lake evaporating from the rising heat; and it is also the rising sap or waters of life up the stems of plants. Li makes water rise, the opposite of its natural tendency. It is the warmth of the sun which draws the water up and which also is the red warmth which corresponds to the blood in our veins.

Li ☲ , the FIRE, stands for separation of 'above' and 'below' like the separation of firmaments and the crux of the turning wave. It is the 'eye' or central opening of the vortex turning and corresponds to the eye in the human body, according to the Chinese system.

Li is the eye that focuses everything into great turning. This is the single eye which unites the double eyes. The single eye is the open yin line in the center which is aware by intuition rather than sensorial seeing. It is clairvoyance, clarity itself. The two eyes lag behind the one central eye like the arms of a galaxy turning around the 'black hole' in the center. The 'black hole' has direct knowledge of anti-universes and the Whole. That which separates the firmaments also unites them, but only through nothingness, no-thing. Li has darkness and vacuity in the center of turning lights, like the pupil set in the iris of the eye. It is through the pupil that the eye sees.

In the water-cycle, the arousing THUNDER of Chen ☳ , is the formation and turbulence of the clouds and their thunderous release of charges towards the earth. Chen is the clapping meeting of wave with the returning wave and the consequent break-up and turbulence. In the Chinese system, it corresponds to the human foot, the great mover. Simultaneously the foot holds the imprint of the whole body as does the iris of the eye. Motion is at its peak in Chen and therefore it polarizes into the release of the THUNDER CLOUDS into wind, rain and lightning.

The penetrating WIND of Sun ☴ corresponds to the

spray or dispersal of the water droplets of the wave-cycle. In the Chinese system, Sun corresponds to the thighs of the human body which are the center of the dance of love. The release in sexual orgasm is relevant here and the motion that is Sun is like the receptacle of all the previous four trigrams, and is itself the source of the following three trigrams. Sun is thus a pivot point of change. The thighs are also the legs as limbs, the movers of the whole body.

The abysmal WATER of K'an ☵, which means sinking,

falling and represents the deep flows of water to lower and lower levels, is a very yin trigram. In the water-cycle, it represents all the downward flow of rivulets, rivers, waterfalls, streams through gorges and open valleys. K'an is like the water of the wave sinking into the sand as the foamy froth gathers in the still moving wave front to the shore, after it has broken. K'an is to be found in all branching and swirling rivulets, moving towards their end. In the Chinese system, K'an corresponds to the ear with its semi-circular canals and receptacle of vast ranges of pure vibration terminating in the cochlea. Complementary to the vortex of Li, the awareness of K'an is on the periphery; whereas in Li, the awareness is through the center.

Consequently the vibratory energy of vortexes is here experienced out on the rim, or the great turning wheels of life. K'an is like the eddies and currents of one thing moving with another. The awareness is in the boundaries, like gears interlocking. Consequently K'an is a good mixer. It is a synthesizer and a solvent. Hard edges are eroded by K'an and it unites what otherwise might remain apart.

It is through time that K'an is known, for time is like the turning of wheels within wheels creating orbits of specific frequencies. Hearing is also a time-dominated process. The eye of Li sees 'all at once,' but the ear hears in sequence. Music and speech take time and are effects of pure vibration.

Li and K'an, the FIRE and WATER, are the main trigrams focalizing the polarity through vortexes. Li, the clear FIRE of solar energy, has resistance outside and is open in the center; whereas K'an, the abysmal WATER of lunar energy, is open, mixing and dissolving on the periphery and is resistant in the core. This dual complementarity of Li and K'an is the secret of the alchemy of the *I Ching* in its final hexagrams of 63 AFTER

COMPLETION and 64 BEFORE COMPLETION.

Ken ≡≡ is the trigram of the still MOUNTAIN. It is

found in the extent of the foam of a wave and where the branching rivulet has reached its end. With Ken we begin the 'backward flowing motion' back to the sea. Ken is also like the underground water in caves and wells and in invisible caverns where the water can go no further.

In the Chinese system, Ken corresponds to the hand, that dexterous extension which can handle many things and yet which is really a pivot point for the motions it initiates all around. The meditation mudras of the hands might be associated with the KEEPING STILL quality of Ken.

Ken also corresponds to the seed (sperm and egg), the termini of birth and death. This is the limit and cessation of a cycle.

With K'un ≡≡, the receptive EARTH, the cycle is

completely backward turning. The light has become darkness. Time ceases and space is the vast vacuum wherein all things are consumed before returning to their source. K'un corresponds to the great sea in the water-cycle and the depths of the earth in landscape. In the sea, all the waters have descended into the vast reservoir of life. Here is the return of the wave to the sea through the sand, through the force of gravity.

We think of gravity operating with great solid masses – stellar and planetary bodies – but it is not the massiveness which 'causes' the gravity; rather the masses are resistances to returning through the 'black hole' at the core of the great void, or to anti-matter. Thus gravity is a force of space rather than of masses.

This is why the trigram of K'un is mysterious and seemingly contradictory. For it is given the attribute of earth which we think of as solid, but also of the receptacle which is openness, a vacuum or space. K'un represents the pole of emptiness, of pure space, darkness and the void, and is the receptacle of the whole cycle of eight trigrams just described. Thus K'un is very vast.

Like the force of gravity, there is no limit to the powers of K'un, vast as infinite space, but its effect is known only through resistances of all the other qualities. The pole of the creative HEAVEN is as needed and as powerful as the pole of the receptive EARTH. They need each other. Every 'solid' planet or star is a ball of interacting resistances which accumulate through the foci of the trigrams in the vacuity of space which is

K'un. All resistances have a two-fold direction: to collapse into the void, into the core of every atom; and to interact with and dominate other entities. It is through this separation and duality that the whole dance becomes possible.

It is Ch'ien and K'un, the creative HEAVEN and the receptive EARTH, which initiate and fulfill the whole cycle. K'un corresponds to the belly, the womb, wherein all things are returned for assimilation and rebirth. Just as the sea is the great receptacle of the landscape, the belly is the great receptacle of the human body. It is the 'water of life' drawn back into the source of the wave. K'un is the nourisher, just as the solar plexus and involuntary nervous system are the nourisher of the brain. Without it, we could neither see nor think, eat nor drink.

K'un is the womb, which is the nourisher of the growing foetus. K'un is the nourisher of the stomach and digestive system and all the cells of the body. It is the nourisher as the sea is the nourisher of all life on earth. And it is the nourisher as the darkness of space is the great womb and belly of all the stars and planets whirling around within it. K'un is the nourisher as life is the nourisher of both birth and death. And it is through the emptiness and weakness and vulnerability of K'un that form and light, the strength and power of Ch'ien, the creative HEAVEN, are again emanated from the blinding light of the source.

This reversal through the basic and primal polarity of Ch'ien, the creative HEAVEN, and K'un the receptive EARTH, happens instantaneously. It takes no time. Like the north and south poles of the planet rotating on its axis, they exist simultaneously, but the awareness of one or the other may be focused at either pole.

K'un is like the cross of life wherein one experiences one's weaknesses, but it is also the power of darkness and space. Ch'ien is like the eternal circle of life wherein one experiences one's strength, but its vulnerability is in the use of power. Focalizing power anywhere is an emanation or radiation whereby it is lessened through the cycles of the trigrams we have just described. It is like wealth. If you have a lot of riches, you must give them out in one form or another or live in fear of being robbed. This is the yang quality of Ch'ien as the creative source. When you have no wealth, there is no fear and the inner freedom and riches can then be very great. This is K'un as the receptive.

Commentary 5
The golden hexagrams

The Golden Hexagram method is an extension of the original *I Ching* in so far as it uses the same basic principles, arriving at the same sixty-four hexagrams, but gives a more transparent view of change. This is due to the fact that the hexagrams themselves have a tendency to change, as well as the usual oracular method whereby one hexagram changes into another hexagram. The Golden Hexagram method condenses the hexagram into an essential 'trigram' form, which, by the principles of the *I Ching*, reveals the changing tendency of the hexagram.

It is by means of the four younger and older ying and yang lines that the *I Ching* hexagrams are realized in their triple essential nature as Heaven-Man-Earth (see Appendix 1).

Each couplet of lines (1 & 2, 3 & 4, 5 & 6) is thereby reduced to its unchanging and changing form of the Golden Hexagrams. You will see in the right-hand corner of each image the changing Golden Hexagram form and its inherent change.

−×− = (yin changing to yang)

−○− = (yang changing to yin)

− − = (unchanging yin)

In the golden hexagrams the lines may be any one of the four types of line: —— pure yang; − − pure yin; −○− changing yang; −×− changing yin; derived from $\equiv$; $\equiv\equiv$; $\equiv\equiv$; and $\equiv\equiv$.

When the *I Ching* hexagrams are reduced by the four kinds of couplets to the golden hexagrams, there are eight out of the total of sixty-four which are immutable (unchanging). These are 1 THE CREATIVE, 34 THE POWER OF THE GREAT, 61 INNER TRUTH, 19 APPROACH, 33 RETREAT, 62 HUMBLE VIGILANCE, 20 CONTEMPLATION and 2 THE RECEPTIVE.

All the other fifty-six golden hexagrams are transformations of one of these eight into another one of the eight. There are twenty-eight pairs which change into each other, revealing a close link of transformation between the two (see Figure B).

The eight immutable golden hexagrams contain the eight qualities of the eight trigrams which correspond in form:

Chien, THE CREATIVE, corresponds with 1 THE CREATIVE.

Tui, THE JOYOUS, corresponds with 34 THE POWER OF THE GREAT.

Li, THE CLINGING, corresponds with 61 INNER TRUTH.

Chen, THE AROUSING, corresponds with 19 APPROACH.

Sun, THE GENTLE, corresponds with 33 RETREAT.

K'an, THE ABYSMAL, corresponds with 62 HUMBLE VIGILANCE.

Ken, KEEPING STILL, corresponds with 20 CONTEMPLATION.

K'un THE RECEPTIVE, corresponds with 2 THE RECEPTIVE.

GOLDEN HEXAGRAMS

They are called golden because the aim of this method of the *I Ching* is an alchemical union of the Tiger and Dragon or feminine and masculine energies which are identified with the

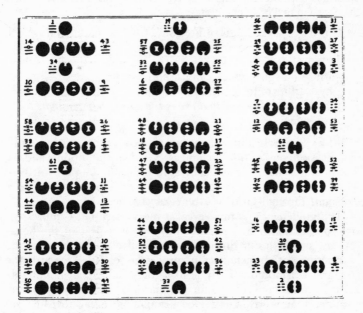

Figure B *The eight immutable golden hexagrams (shown singly) and the twenty-eight pairs of changing golden hexagrams (shown in two stages of change).*

eight immutable hexagrams. According to Taoist yoga, the yin and yang are to be reintegrated through an alchemical (physical, psychological and spiritual) purification through fire (Tiger) and water (Dragon) (see Commentaries 6–8).

After describing the 'seven fires which come from Prenatal Vitality' (pp. 60–1 *Taoist Yoga* by Lu K'uan Yu), the Taoist Master Chao Pi Ch'en relates:

> The above seven kinds of fire come from prenatal vitality and can sublimate all in and out breaths in order to contribute to the manifestation of original spirit. This original spirit is the spirit of no spirit which can use spiritual fire to destroy its (physical) form to return to nothingness in order to achieve immortality. *This spiritual fire is the spirit's golden light that then appears.*

Gold is symbolically the essential extract of wisdom and compassion out of life's changes. Gold is immutable and of inestimable value. Alchemically gold means finding the intrinsic golden thread from the core of one's own being which is a *constant* through all the currents of change.

The golden hexagrams reveal a more essential, compressed, micro-structured, transparent and nuclear aspect of the hexagrams, suited to our times. They are called golden because the extraction of transmutation processes of life toward the Integral Harmonious Body is like gold. Gold is an immutable metal, considered the main standard of currency in many countries. Similarly, the golden hexagrams reveal how fifty-six mutable hexagrams are changing aspects of eight immutable hexagrams constituting the total of sixty-four.

Currency means a flow of value or change. This flow of value must have a standard to back it up or it would not be valuable. The eight unchanging hexagrams are this standard in the *I Ching* of the golden hexagrams. They demonstrate all the possibilities of yin and yang lines in three positions pertaining to Earth-Man-Heaven, analogous to Body-Psyche-Spirit.

In this Commentary we will analyze the qualities of the triple lines pertaining to Earth-Man-Heaven, analogous to Body-Psyche-Spirit.

EARTH: THE BOTTOM LINE OF THE
GOLDEN HEXAGRAMS

When the first and second lines fuse or 'marry' they are combined as the bottom lines of the golden hexagrams.

The bottom two lines are 'seeds' of the potentiality of the future. The lower line is considered the 'beginning'. This is a seed condition which is the result of deep past accumulations of life process. In the case of human beings, it is a deposit of karmic patterns or tendencies towards future thoughts and actions. In this sense the lower two lines are also the past. They are like seeds within the fruit of a tree.

In the golden hexagrams the bottom line may be any one of the four types of line:———pure yang;— —pure yin; —○— changing yang; —×— changing yin, derived from ═══ ; ═ ═ ; ═══ ; and ═ ═.

Pure yang is like a *source* in an explicate or manifest phase. It is like the radiation of a star or sun or the genetic code within the seed. It is *giving, emanating, expanding and full*.

Pure yin is an *effect* in an explicate or manifest phase. It is like the fruit which has absorbed all the qualities of the plant and brought them to fruition. It is analogous to the darkness of space, *receiving, absorbing, all-embracing*.

In an implicate or invisible phase, pure yang is an *effect*. It is the deposits of the radiations it sent out, returning invisibly in the unconscious mind and body. And pure yin is a *source*, being the emanator of essences like the scent, taste and subtle essence of a fruit. Yin in this case is irradiating like an offering of a creature back to the creator. Reciprocity as a sacrifice reveals yin as a giving up of something gross for something subtle.

In human experience, yang in the bottom line of a golden hexagram is extremely subtle vibratory sensations experienced throughout the body. Yin is the sensation of more gross tingling, pain, itching, dullness, cold, etc.

Yin line changing to yang, —×—, implies a change from receiving to giving, non-being to being, desire to fear, or craving to aversion, depending on the attachment or detachment involved.

Yang changing to yin, —○—, implies a change from giving to receiving, fear to desire, radiation to encompassing, being to non-being, etc., depending on the attachment or detachment of

the polarity of sensations of life and the awareness of same.
Through awareness and acceptance of past tendencies, there is
a natural change or transmutation.

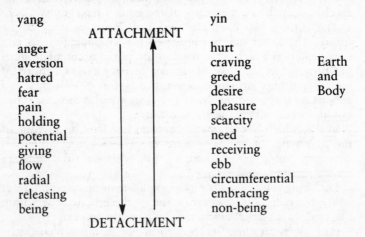

yang		yin	
	ATTACHMENT		
anger		hurt	
aversion		craving	Earth
hatred		greed	and
fear		desire	Body
pain		pleasure	
holding		scarcity	
potential		need	
giving		receiving	
flow		ebb	
radial		circumferential	
releasing		embracing	
being		non-being	
	DETACHMENT		

The body is a deposit of unconscious tendencies that on
surfacing become *sensation*, which is the base of awareness of
one's physical body and karmic tendencies.

Consequently the oracle can be interpreted on many levels,
depending on the degree one has transmuted the gross
sensations into subtle ones. This change depends fundamentally
on quietude, serenity of mind or equanimity amidst the
changing conditions of life.

*It does not so much matter what happens to one as how one
responds to what happens.* If one reacts, there is further
attachment (either by craving or aversion) and an entanglement
in the destructive fires. If one is non-reactive, but serene, then
true action may be taken as the reciprocity of flow and ebb,
giving and receiving, which enables a happy fluidity of subtle
currents to flow throughout the body.

MUTABLE BODY

The *first and second lines of every hexagram, when fused,
represent the body.* Like all couplets when fused, they may be
the pure yin − −, pure yang −−, or changing yin or yang,
−×− or −○−. The forging process of creating our bodies is

mainly unconscious to us. To transmute base material into a 'golden body' implies great purification, renunciation, lack of fears and desires in the vicissitudes of life. A rare state.

When the bottom line of a golden hexagram is $-\circ-$ or $-\times-$ (changing), it indicates a balancing of the body either towards yin or towards yang. Whichever is more harmonious depends on the need of the body.

The fifty-six changing hexagrams are twenty-eight pairs which change into each other. Thus 37 FAMILY tends to change into 6 CONFLICT and vice versa.

37 FAMILY   6 CONFLICT

When the bottom yin changing line of 37 FAMILY changes into the yang changing line of 6 CONFLICT, the receptive body has become a creative body. This implies more action and expressive flow of energy.

Through attentive awareness of this change without reaction, natural reciprocity of giving and receiving, or right nourishment and activity of the body takes place. Through the experiences of change, the awareness remaining serene, the body becomes more pure.

YIN IMMUTABLE BODY

The four immutable golden hexagrams which are pure yin in the bottom line are 2 RECEPTIVE, 20 CONTEMPLATION, 62 HUMBLE VIGILANCE and 33 RETREAT. They all imply keeping the body still or quiet in some sense.

33 RETREAT is an intentional effort to become still after entanglements of life. The body is agitated and one must discipline it to be still. 62 HUMBLE VIGILANCE is becoming humble and peaceful enough to become still, but thoughts are still active, impelling one to move. 20 CONTEMPLATION is a depth of concentration and awareness so that it is no longer so much of an effort to keep the body still. Finally 2 RECEPTIVE is such a calmness and harmony and relaxed receptivity that the body can move without disturbing the quietude of the body.

To take our example of 37 FAMILY again, it consists of the golden hexagram of 20 CONTEMPLATION changing into 1 CREATIVE. This is a dramatic change, from the depth of concentration of the mind so that the body is thoroughly still (sitting in the 'tree' of enlightenment), changing into the body which is dynamic and creatively active even when it is still!

YANG IMMUTABLE BODY

The four immutable golden hexagrams which are pure yang in the bottom line have an active or dynamic aspect in contrast to those of yin which are still. The immutable golden hexagrams which reveal the movement of the body are 1 CREATIVE, 34 POWER OF THE GREAT, 61 INNER TRUTH and 19 APPROACH.

19 APPROACH is the consciously willed effort to move physically towards a goal. 61 INNER TRUTH implies a movement or active effort to overcome outworn habits according to the wisdom of the heart. It is not easy to make these movements because the inertia of the forging of the body from the past tendencies is very great. INNER TRUTH Is a new, fresh insight by which new postures, movements, actions in life are introduced.

The 34 POWER OF THE GREAT implies an overcoming of the habitual tendencies and more powerful ability to move into newness and creative flow, *with intention*. 1 CREATIVE is the spontaneous creative dynamic movement which occurs from attunement of the body to the power of the cosmos even when the body is still!

Thus 20 CONTEMPLATION changing to 1 CREATIVE (as in 37 FAMILY) in the bottom line of the golden hexagram implies a still contemplative body changing into pure creative energy in the flow or currents of energy in the body itself itself. It is intention and discipline becoming spontaneous. As one witnesses this change with reaction (either positive or negative), the yin and yang principles are allowed to change and flow without hindrance and gradually the body is totally relieved of tension, making possible the Harmonious Integral Body or 'Golden Body'.

MAN: THE MIDDLE LINE OF THE GOLDEN HEXAGRAMS

The third and fourth lines, when fused in the golden hexagrams, are the unifiers of the upper and lower trigrams. The fourth line is interpreted as an official, son or woman whereas the third line, being the top of the lower trigram, is an authoritative line.

In the golden hexagrams, the third and fourth lines are fused as the middle line. This is identified with the psyche (both soul and mind) as consciousness. The place of the third line is considered strong whereas that of the fourth is weak. The uniting of the two trigrams in the middle is the role of the psyche. The strength of the third line is movement upward. The weakness of the fourth line is in being a subordinate to the fifth line which is an official or leader.

The psyche may be clear or obscure. These are the two extremes of the pure yin and pure yang lines in the middle of the golden hexagrams. Pure yang is a projective mind as imagination. At its worst, it is delusion, and at its best it is objective vision or prophecy. Pure yin is receptive mind as memory. At its worst, it is forgetting or prejudice, and at its best, it is objective remembering of the deepest past.

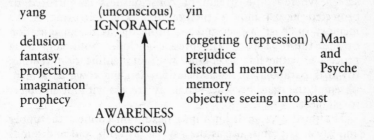

yang	(unconscious)	yin	
	IGNORANCE		
delusion		forgetting (repression)	Man
fantasy		prejudice	and
projection		distorted memory	Psyche
imagination		memory	
prophecy		objective seeing into past	
	AWARENESS		
	(conscious)		

The psyche as consciousness perceives time as past, present and future, but direct experience is always present. Past is stored in memory and future is projected as imagination. Pure awareness of psyche includes past and future.

A changing yin −×− *in the middle line of a golden hexagram is a change from memory to imagination; whereas a changing yang* −○− *is the reverse.* Pure awareness looks both ways: past and future from the present. Ignorance obscures and distorts the past and future or forgets altogether.

In the middle line of golden hexagrams, $-\times-$ is memory which is a future-oriented consciousness and receptivity becoming projective. $-\circ-$ is imagination which is past-oriented, becoming accumulative and contemplative.

The psyche feeds on images and the relations of signs or patterns. Imagination is a formative process of juxtaposing forms and images and relations of signs. Memory is a recollective and recognizing process of forms and images. But pure awareness is neither projective (imagining) or remembering, but includes both. Fluidity of consciousness is a sign of great awareness. Rigid consciousness seeks to cling to one form or another or even to cling to no form.

MUTABLE
PSYCHE

The third and fourth lines of hexagrams, fused, become the mirror of the mind. They are the 'golden' mirror by a similar process as that by which the body becomes 'golden'. The 'golden' mirror implies a mind which has an equanimous right view or is free of attachment and aversions. The mind is a screen whereby the stream of consciousness is mirrored or projected like a motion picture film. The mirroring is the memory or 'past' aspect and the projecting is the imagination or the 'future' aspect. The present includes both, and by a process of witnessing acceptance without identification (tending towards paranoia) or disassociation (tending towards schizophrenia), the mind becomes serene awareness without an object (or subject).

The third or fourth lines in a hexagram connect the upper and lower trigrams just as the psyche (as both soul and mind) links the spirit with the body. The Chinese call the lower two lines, Earth, the middle two lines, Man, and the upper two lines, Heaven. Man is the link between Heaven and Earth just as 'man' as mind or psyche is the link between body and spirit.

The forging of our minds, like our bodies, is from experiences of intense heat whereby it is then cast into a mold and comes out in a certain pattern with certain tendencies according to our past karma. The reforging of those tendencies takes heat at least as intense as in its creation, and a new mold.

The heat is the intensity of our energy of mind and how we can focus attention. This is called concentration.

Without concentration, nothing is possible. The mold is the inclusiveness or exclusiveness of our awareness. If we are constantly judging and rejecting others, we become more and more separative and fragmented in mind. If we are constantly clinging to others and depending on their growth rather than our own, we become more and more vulnerable to the inevitable rejection when they fail, again creating a fragmented mind.

When there is a changing middle line of the golden hexagrams, the yin or yang balancing is a tendency towards memory or imagination. At worst, it is forgetting and delusion. At best, it is objective awareness of past tendencies and prophetic seeing into the future, a true visionary.

YIN IMMUTABLE
PSYCHE

The four immutable golden hexagrams with yin in the middle line are 2 RECEPTIVE, 20 CONTEMPLATION, 19 APPROACH and 61 INNER TRUTH. These four are aspects of stilling or concentrating the mind. 61 INNER TRUTH indicates a psyche who is totally searching for the 'heart of the matter.' All yin aspects of the psyche seek only receptivity, an open state like a question or a probing of memory. 61 INNER TRUTH is a decided effort and intention of mind to encompass and know the truth of the issue.

In 19 APPROACH the psyche has clearly focused and concentrated the mind which is directed to deeply-hidden tendencies of the mind. Questions are aroused, but the mind still has difficulty in equanimity because there are too many questions and often frightening or distracting thoughts coming to the surface.

In 20 CONTEMPLATION all the superfluous questions drop away by means of a more equanimous witnessing of the stream of consciousness. There may still be a tendency to sleep or forget. If one can stay awake, only the biggest, clearest, most pointed question is left, such as 'Who am I?'

Finally in 2 RECEPTIVE, the question is dissolved in pure open awareness and serenity of a completely *golden mirror mind*. There is no object of attention, and no effort. The RECEPTIVE psyche is effortless awareness.

To take our example of 37 FAMILY again, the middle yin line (as CONTEMPLATION) is changing to yang (as CREATIVE), changing the whole golden hexagram into 6 CONFLICT. This is a change of psyche as mind, from the pointed question of equanimous witnessing to spontaneous creative flow.

YANG IMMUTABLE
PSYCHE

The four immutable golden hexagrams with yang in the middle line, corresponding with the psyche, are 1 CREATIVE, 34 POWER OF THE GREAT, 33 RETREAT AND 62 HUMBLE VIGILANCE.

In 62 HUMBLE VIGILANCE we have the dynamic aspect of mind whereby imaginative solutions to questions are sought. The mind is not equanimous enough nor concentrated enough to have clarity. This is sometimes an agitated, confused mind and an alternation of reason and intuition with doubt about either! 62 HUMBLE VIGILANCE is a time to make a large intentional effort to watch the thoughts and feelings without reaction.

33 RETREAT is an effort to witness the mind by conscious volition. The mind is active and one cannot control it, so one must simply watch it. Projections may be frequent. But the serene witnessing is a process which truly breaks the bonds of the wandering mind.

In 34 POWER OF THE GREAT one may direct the mind to actual solutions to problems. Here is creative imagination actively used with will. Volition is used to deliberately conjure up imaginative possibilities. This is the source of magic.

Only in 1 CREATIVE is imagination also dissolved and purely spontaneous insight results. This is not conjurations or fantasies, but insights into the cosmos and oneself. The greatest human discoveries, insights and artistic creations come from this CREATIVE level of mind. Spontaneity, clarity and purity are its qualities without desire or attachment to the result.

You might ask why, then, in 37 FAMILY, where there is a change from 20 CONTEMPLATION to 1 CREATIVE, does it result in 6 CONFLICT? All of the seven golden hexagrams which change into 1 CREATIVE are difficult. The change to the CREATIVE (and the RECEPTIVE) *is like a quantum leap*

of awareness, from separation to pure being and awareness.
The 'I' dissolves.

The reaction to this tendency is 6 CONFLICT. The non-reaction only is CREATIVE. This is because although 37 FAMILY is a change with a tendency towards 6 CONFLICT and CONFLICT back to FAMILY, this pendulum swing can be stopped by pure detached awareness.

HEAVEN: THE TOP LINE OF
THE GOLDEN HEXAGRAMS

The consciousness of the psyche, indicated by the middle line of the golden hexagrams, is a reflection f the awareness of the true Self (top line) on the screen of the mind. The true Self is both wisdom and compassion.

The fifth and sixth lines of the hexagrams, when fused, become the top line of the golden hexagrams. The fifth line is the place of the authoritative official and the sixth line is the place of the sage. The official is the ruler of the hexagram and, together with the sage, represents the master within oneself.

Imagination and memory, future and past projections of the mind are still only on the screen of consciousness. The pure light of awareness is the true Self, but it cannot be seen without a screen to project on.

The body and deep unconscious tendencies are time-bound and constantly going through changes of growth and disintegration. The psyche is time-bound as consciousness projecting future and remembering past, always changing.

The relative source of awareness as the true Self is also changing as a creative center of being. This creative center has a polarity of qualities which are more subtle than either body or mind. The top line of the golden hexagrams concerns the birth and death of the ego and the continuity of the true Self or individuality.

The creative center of being as the true Self is pure awareness of the *mutual arising* of identity and non-identity and thus of the wisdom of knowing that others are not separate from self. The ruler and sage of the fifth and sixth lines are at best wisdom and compassion fused. The I as ego is dissolved, not in unconsciousness, but in pure awareness. This is like the golden sun sending out rays infinitely and indiscriminatingly to one and all without thought of reward or return. This golden sun reflects

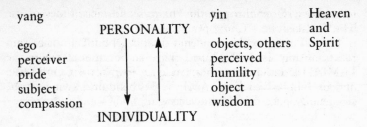

on the screen of consciousness of the psyche as a golden mirror, supported by the radiating and encompassing physical body.

sage (sixth line)	⎫ Golden sun = Heaven
ruler (fifth line)	⎬ of spirit
official, son or woman (fourth line)	⎱
lower ruler (third line)	⎰ Mirror of psyche = Man
lower official (second line)	⎱ Physical body = Earth
beginning situation (first line)	⎰

The body is represented by the symbol of the Earth, the consciousness by Man and pure awareness of the true Self by Heaven.

Chapter X of the *Ta Chuan*, the Great Treatise (p. 377, Wilhelm), says:

1   The Changes is a book vast and great, in which everything is completely contained. The tao of heaven is in it, the tao of earth is in it, and the tao of man is in it. It combines these three primal powers and doubles them; that is why there are six lines. The six lines are nothing other than the ways (tao) of the three primal powers.
2   The Way has changes and movements. Therefore the lines are called changing lines. The lines have gradations, therefore they represent things. Things are diverse; this gives rise to line characteristics. The line characteristics do not always correspond. From this arise good fortune and misfortune.

When the awareness of Heaven is golden, the mirror of the psyche is golden and the body too is golden. This is the Wu Wei, 'doing by non-doing', of the 'superior man'. Ultimately the manifest realm of the changes of the triple world is not different from the unmanifest pure quiescence of Wu Chi. This is so in reality, but not in actuality, and it is the constancy of love and wisdom through the changes and vicissitudes of life which makes the *I Ching* practical.

The self and world appear and disappear, but cannot be said to have being. This is the appearance and disappearance of the Tiger and Dragon as love and wisdom. For in their pure state, neither compassion nor wisdom is of this world. Yet without this changing world and our changing bodies and minds, they would have no meaning for human beings.

The appearance of the Tiger is radiating prophetic compassion. The appearance of the Dragon is encompassing deep memory as wisdom. The disappearance of the Dragon is total fusion with the disappearance of the Tiger. This is receiving the wholeness of compassion, loving others as oneself. This is giving the wholeness of wisdom, knowing others as oneself.

MUTABLE
SPIRIT

The fifth and sixth lines of hexagrams fused become the spirit or essence of the source of 'gold' like the 'golden' sun shining on the mirror of the mind and condensing as the 'golden' body. The ultimate here is compassion-wisdom as an all-embracing awareness. The root of the issue is the 'I' and 'not I,' for by awareness of the whole apparent continuity of life from birth to death do we realize there is no substantial ego. What before one was born and what after death? And even if we take it into previous incarnations and a view of our potential, there is no point at which one can say, 'This is I.' Yet there is a non-thinking direct experience of the true Self.

YIN IMMUTABLE
SPIRIT

Wisdom and compassion are the result of the life of the spirit as it moves through changes. The four immutable golden hexagrams which have yin in the top line (of HEAVEN or spirit) are 2 RECEPTIVE, 62 HUMBLE VIGILANCE, 19 APPROACH and 34 POWER OF THE GREAT. In all four yin aspects there is an emptiness or void of being. Call it non-being. It is the increasing glimpse into the non-reality of the personality and all self-images.

In 34 POWER OF THE GREAT the view into the voi‹

creates a fear of loss of the ego or cherished self-images. It is a first big dip into the void when the mind has revealed a witnessing and detachment to the bring of being 'nobody.' 19 APPROACH is an actual sinking into the emptiness of pure spirit wherein the personality is being stripped, but the perceived and perceiver are still hanging on out of some fear of loss. One is being approached by the spirit to sacrifice self-images.

In 62 HUMBLE VIGILANCE the subject-object division is being severed and dissolved by the humbling experience of the sinking into the void or emptiness. Buddhists call the void shunyata. But in HUMBLE VIGILANCE there are still doubts.

Only at 2 RECEPTIVE is the ego dissolved and no longer do fear and doubts enter. *The void is not experienced as a loss but as the fullness of reality.* 'When spirit and vitality return to this cavity spiritual vitality will soar up to form a circle (of light) which is not void. Voidness which does not radiate is relative but voidness which radiates is absolute' (p. 3, *Taoist Yoga*, Lu K'uan Yu).

The self-images are no longer in the way and reality is just as it is, revealed as devoid of permanent substance in either mind or matter. Spirit is everywhere but totally intangible and in this experience the realization of the divinity of all beings is clear. This is the birth of wisdom.

> The union of spirit and vitality produces the immortal seed as revealed by the white light in the heart, lights flashing in the head, the dragon's hum and the tiger's roar in the ears. If the light of ambrosia is not full and bright, this is due to lack of instruction and guidance by enlightened masters. In this event inner fire should be gathered and lifted to produce spiritual fire which will emit the golden light, and then the light of ambrosia will be full and bright (p. 115, *Taoist Yoga*, Lu K'uan Yu).

YANG IMMUTABLE
SPIRIT

The four immutable golden hexagrams with yang in the top line are 1 CREATIVE, 61 INNER TRUTH, 33 RETREAT and 20 CONTEMPLATION. These four reveal the fullness of being as unique individuality.

20 CONTEMPLATION is the experience of others as oneself but there is still a separation within oneself of personality and individuality.

33 RETREAT is a deepening of this experience so that the 'other' is clearly no longer an object of manipulation by the personality.

In 61 INNER TRUTH, deep spiritual experiences are known whereby the 'marrow' of the true Self is deeply touched in oneself. This enables one to have true compassion and gratitude.

In 1 CREATIVE, compassion and gratitude are a spontaneous overflowing of the plenum of one's true Self pervading one's entire being. This clarity of integration enables one to appreciate the distinct individuality of each through the compassionate awareness that, at the ground of being, there is no separation.

The top line of the golden hexagrams reveals the four-fold pattern of the Mayayana Heart Sutra where it is said,

> O Shariputra, form does not differ from emptiness;
> Emptiness does not differ from form.
> That which is form is emptiness;
> That which is emptiness, form.

Shunryu Suzuki Roshi made the calligraphy of this formula of the Heart sutra during a conversation I had with him in his garden at Tassajara Zen Mountain Center in 1969:

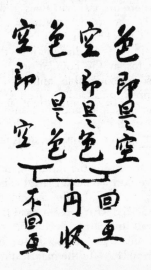

Commentary 6
The derivation of the Tiger and Dragon symbolism

When Li is doubled in hexagram 30, (CLINGING, HARMONY, FLAMING BEAUTY, FIRE) then we have the hexagram which represents the Tiger in Taoist yoga. When K'an is doubled in hexagram 29 (ABYSMAL, SINKING, CHAOS, WATER) then we have the hexagram which represents the Dragon in Taoist yoga.

When we find the immutable aspects of these two hexagrams, we see 30, Li = ☲ = ☲ > ☷

The Tiger, which is the feminine principle, is the transformation of the golden hexagram of 33 RETREAT ䷠ into 34 POWER OF THE GREAT ䷡ wherein there are two yang lines and one yin line.

When K'an is doubled in 29, the hexagram relating to the Dragon, or masculine principle, results in: ☵ = ☵ >

☷ wherein there are two yin lines and one yang line.

The Dragon is the transformation of 19 APPROACH changing into 20 CONTEMPLATION.

To interpret this gives us insight into the process of inner alchemy which aims at the copulation of the Tiger and the Dragon, otherwise irreconcilable 'animals'.

The Tiger is first concealed in RETREAT like the quiet, receptive feminine principle, and then shows its power. In the Taoist yoga diagram for a man, this is the Shen in the head as RETREAT ䷠ (inner vision) circulating down through the

Ch'i and Ching back up to the middle gate of the Chia Chi in the back where we find 34 POWER OF THE GREAT: ䷡

In a woman, 33 RETREAT is the power rising up from the base of the spine, and after becoming completely intuitive through the yin qualities in the head, becoming 34 THE POWER OF THE GREAT in the manifest cycle down the front psychic meridian.

The Dragon first approaches in undulating, watery and airy coils of arousing energy as the masculine principle, and then, in the vastness of space, is contemplative of all the heavens. Here is the arousal of Ching in the sexual center and abdomen as 19 APPROACH, circulating up the back to the head and down again to the Middle Tan-Ti'en of Ch'i in ☰☰ CON-TEMPLATION.

In a woman, APPROACH is manifest in visions in the head centers and CONTEMPLATION is the rising current up the back meridian towards the purely yin principle of intuition in the RECEPTIVE.

The circulation of these qualities through the subtle currents of Ch'i influences the vibratory quality of the hexagram the oracle brings to the questioner.

The reversal of dominance of yin and yang lines for the Dragon and Tiger is inherent in the fact that both the eight trigrams and the eight immutable hexagrams are tertiary derivations from the pure yang of the Creative principle as the father and the pure yin of the Receptive principle as the mother. Both Creative and Receptive (father and mother) are in the Tiger and Dragon.

	Tiger = Daughters		Dragon = Sons	
	Hexagram	Trigram	Hexagram	Trigram
eldest	33 RETREAT	Sun = WIND daughter	19 APPROACH	Chen = THUNDER son
middle	61 INNER TRUTH	Li = FIRE daughter	62 HUMBLE VIGILANCE	K'an = WATER son
youngest	34 POWER OF THE GREAT	Tui = LAKE daughter	20 CONTEM-PLATION	Ken = MOUNTAIN son

The essence of the Tiger is in the house of fire of the heart as 61 INNER TRUTH; whereas the essence of the Dragon is in the house of water as 62 HUMBLE VIGILANCE in the abdomen and nerve plexus.

Commentary 7
The circulation of Ch'i in men and women

The eight immutable golden hexagrams correspond to centers or vortexes of subtle energy (Ch'i) in the body, according to Taoist yoga. As the polarities are reversed for men and women, the implications of the meanings of the hexagrams are somewhat different for men and women in this system of the *I Ching*.

There are twelve hexagrams attributed to the two central meridians up the back and down the front in the center of the body.

Six of the twelve cyclic hexagrams which are related to the central channel (Tu Mo = channel of control and Jen Mo = channel of function) are immutable golden hexagrams.

The other two are the 'House of Fire' (61 INNER TRUTH) and 'House of Water' (62 HUMBLE VIGILANCE) in the heart and abdomen. These two are in the central thrusting channel, Chung Mo.

The polarities of the Ch'i in the central channel relating to hexagrams from head to generative organ are reversed for men and women. In Figure C we give them in their 'golden' (reduced to trigram) forms.

When we reduce these twelve hexagrams to their golden forms we see that six are changing and six are unchanging.

For a man, the current moves up the back (Tu Mo channel) through 24 RETURN, 19 APPROACH, 11 PEACE, 34 POWER OF THE GREAT, 43 RESOLUTION and up to 1 CREATIVE; whereas for a woman these are the golden hexagrams relating to centers down the front (Jen Mo Channel).

In a man the current moves down (Jen Mo Channel) from 1 CREATIVE through 44 ENCOUNTERING, 33 RETREAT, 12 STANDSTILL, 20 CONTEMPLATION, 23 SPLITTING APART to 2 RECEPTIVE; whereas for a woman these are the golden hexagrams relating to centers up the back (Tu Mo channel).

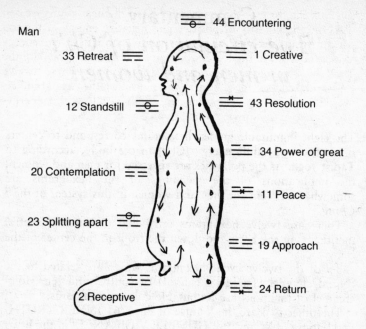

Man

44 Encountering
33 Retreat
1 Creative
12 Standstill
43 Resolution
34 Power of great
20 Contemplation
11 Peace
23 Splitting apart
19 Approach
2 Receptive
24 Return

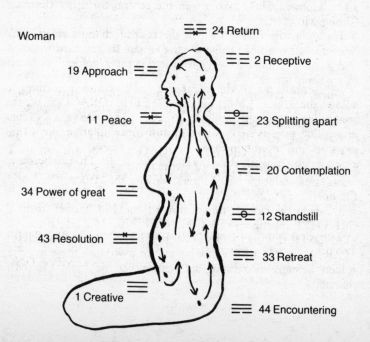

Woman

24 Return
2 Receptive
19 Approach
11 Peace
23 Splitting apart
20 Contemplation
34 Power of great
12 Standstill
43 Resolution
33 Retreat
1 Creative
44 Encountering

From the form of the 'energy-fields' of the hexagrams we can see how the polarity of positive and negative energy at the top of the head 'empties' into the positive and negative energy down the front in the lower abdomen and in turn 'refills' up the back in a man. It is reversed for a woman. These twelve hexagrams reveal most clearly the nature of the hexagrams as 'vessels' which, by emptying and filling, allow the energy-currents to move inward or outward.

DIFFERENCES OF YIN AND YANG
IN MEN AND WOMEN

Since the alchemy of using the Tiger and Dragon Oracle is involved with the union of the masculine and feminine principles within oneself, it is essential to have a clear understanding of the circulation of the Ch'i as it differs for men and women.

For a man, the back is yang and the front is yin, but for woman the front is yang and the back is yin. Also, for the man left is yang and right is yin; whereas for a woman, left is yin and right is yang.

This means that a woman becomes yang in the lower centers whereas a man becomes yang in the head centers. Also, for a woman, yang is a descending cycle towards creative manifestation, whereas for a man, yang is an ascending cycle towards creative ideas.

For a woman, the cycle begins at the base of the spine as the CREATIVE becoming the RETREAT OF THE TIGER. This is a preparation, as in the silence of the feminine principle, to allow the CONTEMPLATION OF THE DRAGON of the masculine principle in her to rise. The DRAGON (her masculine side) is here quiescent and contemplative like a thin mist around mountain-tops.

In STANDSTILL, the RETREAT OF THE TIGER becomes the CONTEMPLATION OF THE DRAGON. Here the masculine and feminine principles within a woman are in balance in the ascending cycle of Ch'i. Being in balance does not mean they are united, but only poised.

The masculine principle within a woman, as the energy ascends, becomes the pure CONTEMPLATION OF THE DRAGON. In the head of a woman the CONTEMPLATING DRAGON polarizes into the purely RECEPTIVE feminine principle through 23 SPLITTING APART. A woman is naturally receptive and open in the head centers to receive inspiration. This is why she tends to be intuitive and 'psychic.'

In woman, as the Ch'i rises to the crown of the head, the RECEPTIVE becomes the APPROACH OF THE DRAGON through 24 RETURN, wherein the yang principle enters. 19 APPROACH is the masculine principle as an active and arousing energy.

A woman then receives a vision of lights or sounds of some intuitive meaning which conveys the possibility of what to manifest or to do next. Her creative aspect is in manifesting; whereas a man's is generally in ideas. As the subtle energy descends down a woman's front meridian there is 11 PEACE, as a balance of the masculine and feminine principles again pose themselves. This is not a fusion, but like a pause or rest after intense interaction. In this PEACE, the POWER OF THE GREAT OF THE TIGER meets the APPROACH OF THE DRAGON. This is experienced in the 'Heavenly Fire of the Heart' chakra wherein peace may truly be found in balance, but with intensity.

In a woman, as the Ch'i descends, the POWER OF THE GREAT OF THE TIGER manifests in the Ch'i or Middle Tan T'ien (solar plexus center). Here is a great reservoir of energy which, in transition to the CREATIVE, awakens the Ching or lower Tan T'ien ('navel' or spleen center) as 43 RESOLUTION. Finally, at the sexual center, the full creative force of pure yang is opened as manifestation for the woman in 1 THE CREATIVE.

The creative force of yang at the sexual center of a woman does not necessarily mean sexual intercourse (although, if both man and woman have developed subtle Ch'i, it may be a 'tantric' union), but indicates a power to manifest according to her vision.

This is a very powerful awakening for a woman, for it indicates the possibility of creating, tangibly, family, culture, the arts, etc. If she has *not* been receptive, intuitive and open to the cosmic order, her vision may be dangerous and she may become militant in the manifesting, descending cycle. Here is one half of the root of war. Man provides the other half.

For women to have clear vision and the power to manifest, indicates intuition in action. This is a union of her masculine and feminine, yang and yin, Dragon and Tiger aspects.

More specifically, as we can see from the diagram of the Ch'i in men and women, the intuition from the RECEPTIVE changes to the APPROACH OF THE DRAGON in the Ni Wan or Top Tan T'ien (third eye), and, as the current descends, it becomes the POWER OF THE GREAT OF THE TIGER and finally the CREATIVE in the sexual center.

All this is contingent upon a woman being able to be quiet and still, to cease all fears and desires, so that as the yin energy rises, she can be totally receptive. The quiet, ascending part of the cycle is as important as the arousing, visionary and actively manifesting part. The former is invisible and contemplative and the latter is visible and socially interactive.

Man is most creative in the head centers which tend towards abstractions, whereas a woman is most creative in the lower centers which tend towards manifestation. The woman must be quiet to receive visions and intuitions of what to do, and the man must be active, initiating and enterprising to bring forth ideas so that, when they are brought forth (sometimes in books or plans, inventions or designs), he can become quiet and contemplative as his energy descends.

This means that it is natural for a woman to put energy into being contemplative and harmonious. Then the manifestation is done almost will-lessly. It is natural for the man to put energy into the formation of ideas, and contemplation and receptivity is done almost will-lessly.

When the masculine and feminine principles unite within a man, the golden hexagram of 63 ䷾ AFTER COM-

PLETION, which is the RECEPTIVITY in the sexual center, becomes the CREATIVE ☰ in the 'Jade Gate' in the head;

and 64 ䷿ BEFORE COMPLETION, which is CREATI-

VITY in the head, becomes the ☷ RECEPTIVE in the

sexual center. For a woman, the golden hexagrams are reversed as we have seen.

Since the human body is a microcosm of the cosmic harmonies and order, through awareness within the body we can also know how it is 'outside.' For the subjective and objective are not separate. Through the practice of the golden hexagrams in the yoga of the 'circulation of the light,' one may realize clearly what to do in daily life.

The two remaining immutable golden hexagrams are the essence of the Tiger and Dragon which in their trigram forms are Li and K'an. As golden hexagrams they are 61 INNER TRUTH and 62 HUMBLE VIGILANCE. These are the 'House of Fire' in the heart and the 'House of Water' in the abdomen and brain.

Commentary 8
Moon-cycles and binary order of hexagrams as currents influencing the tiger and dragon changes

As shown in the chart on page 286, each hexagram in the Tiger and Dragon Oracle corresponds with a phase of the moon-cycle, either from a heavenly view (solar) or from an earthly view.

There are eight 'timeless' pivot points of the moon-cycle. They might be compared to the moment between inhaling and exhaling breaths, wherein motion could neither be said to be going out nor coming in. These eight hexagrams are based on the absolute symmetry of the hexagrams in pairs of opposites and indicate a time to pause and look into the essence of the issue.

Earth view:
2 RECEPTIVE
62 HUMBLE VIGILANCE
29 THE ABYSMAL
28 CRITICAL POINT

Heaven view:
1 CREATIVE
61 INNER TRUTH
30 FLAMING BEAUTY
27 NOURISHMENT

The twenty-eight earthly view moon-cycle hexagrams and their four 'timeless' pivot points represent phases of increasing manifestation from the dark moon of RETURN, after the RECEPTIVE pivot point, to the full moon of UNITY, through the waxing cycle to RESOLUTION, wherein a transition to the heavenly moon-cycles occurs. *The earthly view hexagrams suggest good times to do something outwardly.*

The twenty-eight heavenly view hexagrams and their four 'timeless' points of transition suggest a filling of the vessels of change with yang, creative energy from below, until with the CREATIVE there is cessation. They move from SPLITTING APART just after full moon to GREAT POSSESSIONS at the

inner richness of the heavenly dark moon, and around to
ENCOUNTERING at the full moon whereby the cycle ceases
at the CREATIVE. *The heavenly moon-cycle hexagrams are a
time of reseeding the inner moon elixir, that is regaining a
spiritual influx which is hidden to ordinary vision.* When
drawing these hexagrams it is well to remain quiet and
internally aware.

The moon-cycles are based on the binary order of the
hexagrams which is as follows:

Earthly view of moon-cycles

Binary number	Hexagram number and name	Moon phase
0	2 RECEPTIVE	pivot point
1	24 RETURN	dark moon
2	7 THE ARMY	
3	19 APPROACH	
4	15 MODESTY	
5	36 DARKENING LIGHT	
6	46 PUSHING UPWARD	
7	11 PEACE	
8	16 ENTHUSIASM	waxing half
9	51 THE AROUSING	
10	40 DELIVERANCE	
11	54 MARRYING MAIDEN	
12	62 HUMBLE VIGILANCE	pivot point
13	55 ABUNDANCE	
14	32 DURATION	
15	34 POWER OF THE GREAT	
16	8 UNITY	full moon
17	3 DIFFICULTY AT THE BEGINNING	
18	29 THE ABYSMAL	pivot point
19	60 PROPORTION	
20	39 OBSTRUCTION	
21	63 AFTER COMPLETION	
22	48 THE WELL	
23	5 WAITING	
24	45 GATHERING TOGETHER	waning half
25	17 FOLLOWING	
26	47 OPPRESSION	

27	58 JOYOUS
28	31 INFLUENCE
29	49 REVOLUTION
30	28 CRITICAL POINT
31	43 RESOLUTION

Heavenly view of moon-cycles

Binary number	Hexagram number and name	Moon phase
32	23 SPLITTING APART	
33	27 NOURISHMENT	pivot point
34	4 IMMATURITY	
35	41 DECREASE	
36	52 KEEPING STILL	
37	22 GRACE	
38	18 WORK ON DECAY	
39	26 FORCE OF GREAT	waning half
40	35 PROGRESS	
41	21 BITING THROUGH	
42	64 BEFORE COMPLETION	
43	38 OPPOSITION	
44	56 WANDERER	
45	30 FLAMING BEAUTY	pivot point
46	50 CAULDRON	
47	14 GREAT POSSESSIONS	dark moon
48	20 CONTEMPLATION	
49	42 INCREASE	
50	59 DISSOLVING	
51	61 INNER TRUTH	pivot point
52	53 DEVELOPMENT	
53	37 FAMILY	
54	57 PENETRATING	
55	9 FORCE OF SMALL	waxing half
56	12 STANDSTILL	
57	25 INTEGRITY	
58	6 CONFLICT	
59	10 TREADING	
60	33 RETREAT	
61	13 FELLOWSHIP	
62	44 ENCOUNTERING	full moon
63	1 CREATIVE	pivot point

The significance of the moon-cycles is given at the beginning of each reading of each golden hexagram.

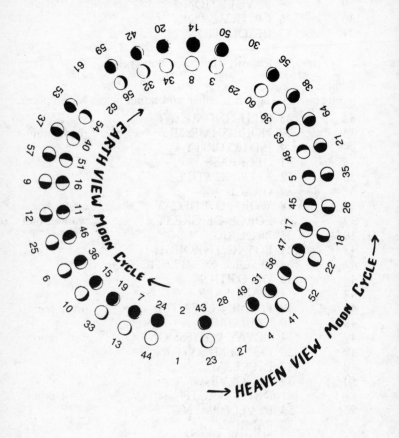

APPENDICES

Appendix 1
Four emblematic figures

We quote at length from the notes of James Legge, quoted by Z.D. Sung in *Symbols of the Yi King*, p.68:

> The other [method] is based on the use of the 'four Hsiang,' or emblematic figures (══ the great or old yang, ═══ the young yang, ══ the old yin, and ══ the young yin).

> Those were assigned the numbers 9, 8, 7, 6. They were 'the old yang' represented by 9, the 'old yin' represented by 6, that in the manipulation of the stalks to form new diagrams, determined the changes of figures; and so 9 and 6 came to be used as the names of a yang line and a yin line respectively. This explanation is now universally acquiesced in.

The four emblematic figures were assigned to the old and young yin and yang with general consensus as follows:

James Legge (p.375, Dover Edition)		Wilhelm/Baynes (p.319)	
═══	grand or old yang (9)	═══	old or great yang
══	young yin (8)	═══	young or little yang
═══	young yang (7)	═══	young or little yin
══	grand or old yin (6)	══	old or great yin

(The number assignments above are Legge's.)

Z.D. Sung (pp.68 and 75)		Hua-Ching Ni (p.26)	
═══	old yang (9)	═══	strong yang
═══	young yang (7)	══	lesser yin

⚊⚊ young yin   (8) ⚎ lesser yang

⚏ old yin   (6) ⚍ strong yin

There is some discrepancy but general concordance except that Wilhelm/Baynes has the young yin and yang reversed from Legge, Ni and Sung.

The symbolism of numbers applies to changing and unchanging lines when, in the coin or stalk method, one hexagram changes into another. However, in the Tiger and Dragon Oracle we are using a contraction of couplets, representing the trinity common through the ancient world of Earth (bottom two lines), Man (middle two lines) and Heaven (top two lines).

This method of contraction should not be confused with the four emblematic figures given above (even though they look the same!). *The changes of the Golden Hexagram method shows the change within any one hexagram and is not a change from one hexagram to another. This method of contraction employed retains the similarity of the eight immutable golden hexagrams and the eight trigrams.*

The assignments are as follows:

⚌ = (unchanging yang)   ⚊   7
⚎ = (yin changing to yang) —×—   6
⚍ = (yang changing to yin) —○—   9
⚏ = (unchanging yin)   ⚋⚋   8

It is this insight into the tendency of change within each hexagram which enables the user of the Tiger and Dragon Oracle to discover the essence or innermost quality in each hexagram.

Appendix 2
Brief history of *I Ching*

We give some idea of the background of the *I Ching* so that we can understand its possible use in modern times.

The composition of the traditional *I Ching* is attributed to King Wen who was the father of the founder of the Chou dynasty (1150–249 BC). He arranged the texts in the manner found in the Wilhelm/Baynes, James Legge, Blofeld and other western translations published in our times. King Wen was widely acclaimed as a culture-hero and virtuous Chinese leader who truly lived the wisdom of the *I Ching*.

The history of the *I Ching* preceding King Wen is less clear because some of it is legendary rather than known from written documents. The culture-hero known as Fu Hsi is said to have devised the elementary 'yin' and 'yang' lines, the Four Emblematic Symbols and the eight trigrams. The legend of Fu Hsi – that he saw the eight trigrams on the back of a tortoise's shell – does establish that the fundamental principles of the *I Ching* go back to an oral tradition thousands of years BC.

According to Hellmut Wilhelm, the *I Ching* was earlier composed of two books. The first book was called Lien Shan, 'Mountains Standing Together,' and is thought to have been written in the Hsia dynasty (2205–1766 BC) and the second book was called Kuei Ts'ang, 'Reverting to the Hidden,' and was used in the Shang dynasty (1766–1150 BC).

Confucius (522–479 BC), and other philosophers of his time and earlier, made commentaries on the Judgments and Images of the earlier *I Ching*. The *I Ching* is listed among the Chinese classics as late as the third century BC, but the commentaries, called the Ten Wings, were likely made much earlier.

The fifth and sixth Wing is called the Great Treaties (Hsi Tz'u Chuan or Ta Chuan) and is the most important for understanding the structure of the *I Ching*. Richard Wilhelm states in his commentaries that the Great Treatise was not made by Confucius, but by late Chou philosophers.

From Han dynasty (206 BC to AD 220) onward the *I Ching*

has had an unbroken continuity of use in China and is ranked as one of the major philosophical classics.

The *I Ching* has come into the European and American cultures slowly. Christian missionaries in China came across it. Father Bouvet, while in Peking, wrote to Leibniz (1646–1716), the German philosopher and mathematician, about the trigrams and hexagrams of the *I Ching*. Leibniz was enthused by the binary arrangement of the *I Ching* as well as its philosophical implications and wrote some articles on it.

James Legge made an English translation in 1854 and Richard Wilhelm rendered the *I Ching* into German in 1924. Since the written characters of the Chinese language are not words, but are ideographs or symbols of ideas, the translation was difficult. The imagistic and metaphorical way of Chinese thinking being very different from the western linear, 'rational' way of thinking since the so-called 'Age of Enlightenment', made interpretation by westerners difficult also.

However, as time went on, western civilization began showing signs of being tired of its overly dominant 'yang' technological development and linear methods of thinking, and sought sources, eastern, aboriginal and ancient, to balance it. For example, in the 1890s the painter Paul Gauguin left civilized France to find an aboriginal quality in the South Seas and many 'impressionists' turned to the japanese wood-cut for inspiration. D.H. Lawrence left cold, reserved and sophisticated England to find the 'Plumed Serpent,' Questzalcoatl, in the Americas, and C.G. Jung explored world-wide symbolisms to find universal qualities of archetypes towards a psychology of wholeness.

In America and Europe, Zen Buddhism and various forms of Hinduism swept through the psyches of people with left-brain fatigue in the 1950s and 60s, and these, along with eastern practices of T'ai Chi Chuan, Hatha Yoga, Aikido and Kung Fu, revealed value changes at work. Vipassana Buddhism and other eastern practices have become influential in the west in the 1970s and 80s.

The *I Ching* appeared on the western scene in 1899 (Legge) in a series called *The Sacred Books of the East* and became more popular when the Wilhelm/Baynes version was published in 1950.

Much of the search of the west was to re-establish a 'yin' balance to an overly 'yang' world wherein the more nurturing feminine, intuitive, metaphorical, nature- and earth-conscious tendencies could flourish. The *I Ching* not only brings an eastern antidote to 'yang' left-brain fatigue, but brings a wholeness which is not merely a reaction of one extreme to another. This wholeness is due to the structure of the *I Ching* itself which is linked with its history and use.

Bibliography

Argüelles, José, 'Compute and Evolve: Some Reflections of the I Ching as a Prelude to a Post-scientific System,' *Main Currents in Modern Thought*, 25 (Jan.–Feb., 1969).

Beau, Georges, *Chinese Medicine*, Avon Books, 1965.

Bernstein, Jeremy, 'A Question of Parity,' *New Yorker*, May 12, 1962.

Bjerregaard, C. H. A., *The Inner Life and the Tao-Teh-King*, Theosophical Pub., 1912.

Blofeld, John, *I Ching*, Dutton Paperback, 1968.

Burke, Kenneth, *Permanence and Change*, Los Altos, Hermes, 1954.

Cammann, Schuyler, 'The Magic Square of Three in Old Chinese Philosophy and Religion,' *History of Religions*, 1, 1961.

Carroll, Thomas D., 'The Hidden Significance of the I-ching Diagrams,' *Journal of the China Society* (Taipei), 2, 1962.

Carus, Paul, *Chinese Astrology*, Open Court, La Salle, Illinois, 1974.

Chang, Chung-Yuan, *Creativity and Taoism – A Study of Chinese Philosophy, Art and Poetry*, The Julian Press, 1963.

Chi-yun, Chang, 'The Book of Changes,' *Chinese Culture* 6, no. 4, (Oct. 1965).

Chu, W. K. and W. E. Sherril, *The Astrology of the I Ching*, Routledge & Kegan Paul, 1976; Samuel Weiser, 1980.

Chu, W. K. and W. E. Sherril, *An Anthology of I Ching*, Routledge & Kegan Paul, 1977.

Cooper, J. C., *Taoism*, Aquarian Press, 1972.

Dhiegh, Khigh, Alx, *The Eleventh Wing: An Exposition of the Dynamics of I Ching for Now*, Los Angeles, Nash, 1973.

Dhiegh, Khigh, Alx, *I Ching: Taoist Book of Days*, Calendar-Diary, 1975, Shambhala, Berkeley, 1974.

Gardner, Martin, 'Mathematical Games: The Combinatorial Basis of the I Ching, The Chinese Book of Divination and Wisdom,' *Scientific American*, Jan. 1974.

Giles, Herbert A., tr., Chuang Tzu: *Mystic, Moralist and Social Reformer*, Kelly and Walsh, Shanghai, 1926; reprinted by AMS press, New York.

Govinda, Lama Anagarika, *The Inner Structure of the I Ching*, Wheelwright Press, 1981.

Hook, Diana ffarington, *The I Ching and You*, Routledge & Kegan Paul, 1973.

Hook, Diana ffarington, *The I Ching and Mankind*, Routledge & Kegan Paul, 1975.

Hook, Diana ffarington, *The I Ching and its Associations*, Routledge & Kegan Paul, 1980.

Huon der Kermadec, Jean-Michel, *The Way to Chinese Astrology; The Four Pillars of Destiny*, Unwin Paperbacks, 1983.

Johnson, Willard, *I Ching: An Introduction to the Book of Changes*, Shambala, Berkeley, 1969.

Kaplan, Charles David, 'Method as Phenomenon: The Case of the *I Ching*,' Master's thesis, University of California Los Angeles, 1973.

Lach, Donalk, 'Leibniz and China,' *Journal of the History of Ideas*, 14 (1945).

Lau, D. C., trans., Lao Tzu, *Tao Te Ching*, Penguin, 1963.

Lee, Jung Young, *The Principles of Changes: Understanding the I Ching*, New Hyde Park, N.Y. University Books, 1971.

Legge, James, trans., *The Yi King, Part 2 of The Sacred Books of China, The Texts of Confucianism*, in *The Sacred Books of the East*, ed. by F. Max Muller, vol. 16, Oxford, Clarendon, 1882.

Legge, James, trans., *The I Ching*, Dover Paperback, 1963.

Mann, Felix, *Acupuncture: The Ancient Chinese Art of Healing and How it Works Scientifically*, Vintage Books, 1973.

McCaffree, Joe E., *Divination and the Historical and Allegorical Sources of the I Ching, The Chinese Classic or Book of Changes*, Miniverse Serves, Los Angeles, 1967.

McEvilly, Wayne, 'Synchronicity and the *I Ching*,' *Philosophy East and West*, 18, no. 3, July, 1968.

Merton, Thomas, *The Way of Chuang Tzu*, New Directions, 1965.

Metzner, Ralph, *Map of Consciousness*, New York, Collier Books, 1971.

Mungello, David E., 'Liebnitz's Interpretation of Neo-Confucianism,' *Philosophy East and West*, 21, no. 1 (Jan, 1971).

Murphy, Joseph, *Secrets of the I Ching*, West Myack, N.Y. Parker, 1970.

Needham, Joseph, 'The System of the Book of Changes; Science and Civilisation in China,' vol. 2, *History of Scientific Thought*, Cambridge University Press, 1956.

Ni, Hua-Ching, *Tao, The Subtle Universal Law and the Integral Way of Life*, Shrine of Eternal Breath of Tao, 1979.

Ni, Hua-Ching, *The Book of Changes and the Unchanging Truth*, Shrine of Eternal Breath of Tao, 1983.

Olsvanger, Immanuel, *Fu-Hsi, the Sage of Ancient China*, Jerusalem, Massadah, 1948.

Pattee, Rowena, *Mapping of Leptons and Quarks on the I Ching*, Energy Unlimited, 1983 (available for $4. c/o Golden Point Productions, P.O. Box 784, Point Reyes Station, CA. 94956).

Ponce, Charles, *The Nature of the I Ching, Its Usage and Interpretation*, Award Books, new York, 1970.

Ritsema, Rudolf, 'Notes for Differentiating Some Terms in the I Ching,' *Spring*, 1970.

Rump, Ariane, *The Darkening of the Light as an Aspect of Evil in the I Ching*, Columbia University, April 1972.

Schonberger, Martin, *The I Ching and the Genetic Code*, A.S.I., 1979.

Siu, R. G. H., *The Man of Many Qualities: A Legacy of the I Ching*, Cambridge, Mass., M.I.T. Press, 1968.

Siu, R. G. H., Ch'i, *A Neo-Taoist Approach to Life*, Cambridge, Mass., M.I.T. Press, 1974.

Sung, Z. D., *The Text of Yi King*, Paragon, 1969.

Sung, Z. D., *The Symbols of Yi King*, Paragon, 1969.

Suzuki, D. T. and Paul Carus, trans., *The Canon of Reason and Virtue*, Open Court, La Salle, Illinois, 1974.

Swanson, Gerald William, 'The Great Treatise: Commentory Tradition of the Book of Changes,' Ph.D. dissertation, University of Washington, 1974.

Tong, Lik Kuen, 'The Concept of Time in Whitehead and the I Ching',' *Journal of Chinese Philosophy*, 1, no. 3/4 (June–Sept. 1974).

Van der Blij, F., 'Combinational Aspects of the Hexagrams in the Chinese Book of Changes,' *Scripta Mathamatica*, 28, no. 1, 1966.

Veith, Izza, *The Yellow Emperor's Classic of Internal Medicine*, University of California Press, 1966.

Waley, Arthur, *The Way and Its Power*, London, Allen & Unwin, 1934.

Waley, Arthur, *Madly Singing in the Mountains*, London, Allen and Unwin, 1970.

Watts, Alan, *Tao and the Watercourse Way*, Pantheon, 1975.

Welch, Holmes, *The Parting of the Way: La Tsu and the Taoist Movement*, Methuen and Co. Ltd., 1957.

Wilhelm, Hellmut, *Change*, Bollingen Fo., 1960.

Wilhelm, Richard, *The I Ching or Book of Changes*, Bollingen Series XIX, 1950.

Wilhelm, Richard, *Lectures on the I Ching*, Bollingen Series XIX, 1979.

Wilhelm, R. and C. G. Jung, *The Secret of the Golden Flower*, Harcourt, Brace and World, 1931.

Wong, S. Y., 'The Book of Change: A New Interpretation,' *Eastern Horizon*, 2 (1962).Yu, Lu K'uan, *The Secrets of Chinese Meditation*, Weiser, 1972.

Yu, Lu K'uan, *Taoist Yoga*, Weiser, 1970.

Yuen, Ko (Aleister Crowley), *Shih Yi: A Critical and Mnemonic Paraphrase of the Yi King*, Oceanside, California, Thelema Publications, 1971.

POSTAL ORDERS

I Ching illustrated Tiger and Dragon cards with full color backs are available for $12 (plus handling-shipping charges: $2 in U.S., $2.75 in Canada and $4.60 in Great Britain).

I Ching Tiger and Dragon posters of all sixty-four hexagrams on four posters are available for $10 (plus handling-shipping charges: $2.25 in U.S.A., $3.00 in Canada and $5.00 in Great Britain).

Send Money Order or Check in U.S. dollars to:

Golden Point Productions
P.O. Box 7
Mount Shasta, CA 96067, U.S.A.

Index

Key for identifying
the hexagrams

UPPER TRIGRAM LOWER TRIGRAM	CHYAN ☰	CHEN ☳	K'AN ☵	KEN ☶	K'UN ☷	SUN ☴	LI ☲	TUI ☱
CHIAN ☰	1	34	5	26	11	9	14	43
CHEN ☳	25	51	3	27	24	42	21	17
K'AN ☵	6	40	29	4	7	59	64	47
KEN ☶	33	62	39	52	15	53	56	31
K'UN ☷	12	16	8	23	2	20	35	45
SUN ☴	44	32	48	18	46	57	50	28
LI ☲	13	55	63	22	36	37	30	49
TUI ☱	10	54	60	41	19	61	38	58

ARKANA – NEW-AGE BOOKS FOR MIND, BODY AND SPIRIT

With over 150 titles currently in print, Arkana is the leading name in quality new-age books for mind, body and spirit. Arkana encompasses the spirituality of both East and West, ancient and new, in fiction and non-fiction. A vast range of interests is covered, including Psychology and Transformation, Health, Science and Mysticism, Women's Spirituality and Astrology.

If you would like a catalogue of Arkana books, please write to:

Arkana Marketing Department
Penguin Books Ltd
27 Wright's Lane
London W8 5TZ

ARKANA – NEW-AGE BOOKS FOR MIND, BODY AND SPIRIT

A selection of titles already published or in preparation

A Course in Miracles: The Course, Workbook for Students and Manual for Teachers

Hailed as 'one of the most remarkable systems of spiritual truth available today', *A Course in Miracles* is a self-study course designed to shift our perceptions, heal our minds and change our behaviour, teaching us to experience miracles – 'natural expressions of love' – rather than problems generated by fear in our lives.

Medicine Woman: A Novel   Lynn Andrews

The intriguing story of a white woman's journey of self-discovery among the Heyoka Indians – from the comforts of civilisation to the wilds of Canada. Apprenticed to a medicine woman, she learns tribal wisdom and mysticism – and above all the power of her own womanhood.

Arthur and the Sovereignty of Britain: Goddess and Tradition in the Mabinogion   Caitlín Matthews

Rich in legend and the primitive magic of the Celtic Otherworld, the stories of the *Mabinogion* heralded the first flowering of European literature and became the source of Arthurian legend. Caitlín Matthews illuminates these stories, shedding light on Sovereignty, the Goddess of the Land and the spiritual principle of the Feminine.

Shamanism: Archaic Techniques of Ecstasy   Mircea Eliade

Throughout Siberia and Central Asia, religious life traditionally centres around the figure of the shaman: magician and medicine man, healer and miracle-doer, priest and poet.

'Has become the standard work on the subject and justifies its claim to be the first book to study the phenomenon over a wide field and in a properly religious context' – *The Times Literary Supplement*

ARKANA – NEW-AGE BOOKS FOR MIND, BODY AND SPIRIT

A selection of titles already published or in preparation

The I Ching and You Diana ffarington Hook

A clear, accessible, step-by-step guide to the *I Ching* – the classic book of Chinese wisdom. Ideal for the reader seeking a quick guide to its fundamental principles, and the often highly subtle shades of meaning of its eight trigrams and sixty-four hexagrams.

A History of Yoga Vivian Worthington

The first of its kind, *A History of Yoga* chronicles the uplifting teachings of this ancient art in its many guises: at its most simple a beneficial exercise; at its purest an all-embracing quest for the union of body and mind.

Tao Te Ching The Richard Wilhelm Edition

Encompassing philosophical speculation and mystical reflection, the *Tao Te Ching* has been translated more often than any other book except the Bible, and more analysed than any other Chinese classic. Richard Wilhelm's acclaimed 1910 translation is here made available in English.

The Book of the Dead E. A. Wallis Budge

Intended to give the deceased immortality, the Ancient Egyptian *Book of the Dead* was a vital piece of 'luggage' on the soul's journey to the other world, providing for every need: victory over enemies, the procurement of friendship and – ultimately – entry into the kingdom of Osiris.

Yoga: Immortality and Freedom Mircea Eliade

Eliade's excellent volume explores the tradition of yoga with exceptional directness and detail.

'One of the most important and exhaustive single-volume studies of the major ascetic techniques of India and their history yet to appear in English' – *San Francisco Chronicle*